Women and Politics in Nagaland

About the Author

Toshimenla Jamir teaches Sociology at the Nagaland University. Besides being an advocate for women's rights, she is a pioneer in the area of Gender Studies in the region. She has contributed in the field through a number of important publications and presentations at international and national levels. She has also co-authored a book 'Process of Land Alienation in Nagaland'.

Women and Politics in Nagaland

Challenges and Imperatives

Toshimenla Jamir

CONCEPT PUBLISHING COMPANY PVT. LTD.
NEW DELHI-110059

ISBN-13-978-81-8069-882-8

First Published 2012

Published and Printed by

Since 1974

Concept Publishing Company Pvt. Ltd.
A/15-16, Commercial Block, Mohan Garden
New Delhi-110059 (India)
T: 25351460, 25351794, *F*: 091-11-25357109
E: publishing@conceptpub.com, W: www.conceptpub.com
Editorial Office: H-13, Bali Nagar, New Delhi-110 015, India.

Cataloging in Publication Data--Courtesy: D.K. Agencies (P) Ltd. <docinfo@dkagencies.com>

Jamir, Toshimenla.
Women and politics in Nagaland : challenges and imperatives / Toshimenla Jamir.
p. cm.
Includes bibliographical references (p.) and index.
ISBN 9788180698828

1. Women—Political activity—India—Nagaland. 2. Naga (South Asian people)—India—Nagaland—Politics and government. I. Title.

DDC 305.420954165 23

CHAIRPERSON
Nagaland State Commission for Women
Kohima - 797 001, Nagaland.

Foreword

Naga society has for a long time been known to be egalitarian in nature, with a balance in gender relationships. And yet recent findings show that this is quite the contrary. On a wider scale gender inequality has been recognised as the most crucial impediment to social development in the 21st century. Hence, the exigency to incorporate women into decision-making institutions and bodies at all levels needs to be addressed. The present work of Toshimenla Jamir has come at the most appropriate time when Naga society stands at the crossroads over this very question of including women in decision-making. The recent High Court ruling on the 33 per cent reservation for women in the Municipal and Town Councils in Nagaland is a major landmark in Naga women's history. The contributions of genuinely concerned women will come from a different angle than what has been the normal, with only men representing the entire society. Such inclusive leadership can bring about a deeper understanding of the society's needs and result in a broader perspective of the social milieu, leading to a society that is more extensively cared for.

Toshimenla Jamir has been thorough in her approach in creating an understanding of the context, and has very succinctly, from an insider's perspective, identified the wide array of challenges facing contemporary Naga women. As well, she has come up with insightful and well-researched suggestions to meet these challenges. To the best of my knowledge, this is a pioneering work in this area from a Naga scholar and it would be an invaluable resource to policy makers, researchers and academicians alike.

Sano Vamuzo

Kohima
November 22, 2011

Preface

The world is today facing both quantitative and qualitative changes—quantitative in terms of economic growth and technological change; qualitative in terms of a new paradigm of a society governed by a new set of values and ethos-gender equality is central to this new paradigm. Nagaland claims to be a women-equivalence society. Is that really the reality or just a myth perpetuated through tall claims of gender-equality seen through the male prism in an otherwise unequal society? Recent reports and studies suggest that the truth may be very far from the claims. Take for instance, the recently released report by the UNDP and the Ministry of Child and Women Development entitled 'Gendering Human Development Indices: Recasting Gender Development and Gender Empowerment Measure for India 2009.' According to this report, on a good number of Gender Empowerment Measure (GEM), Nagaland lags behind States such as Bihar and Orissa. The GEM measured men and women's active participation in political and economic life and their command over economic resources. Of all the thirty-five Union Territories/States, Nagaland and Jammu and Kashmir ranked lowest with a GEM of 0.304 till 2006. This brings into sharp focus the question of women's rights in Naga society. Unfortunately in Naga society today, women empowerment appears to many to be an alien concept, a typically western concept which has no place in Naga society. They perceive talks of women empowerment as threatening the very foundation of Naga society. Perhaps, it is for such reasons that Naga society continue to be steeped in primordial attitude and reasoning which continue to resist the idea of women as equal partners in society. Naga society has a condescending attitude towards its women. It reminds me of an observation made by a respected academician of the region, when she referred to the case of women in Naga society as 'benevolent subordination".* A very apt description indeed.

Even though many legislative measures have been passed in the country, they have failed to make much impact on the life of the Naga women. Despite constitutional provisions, Nagas have been governed by customary laws which have failed to give women their due. Therefore, we can see that Naga women have been living in two types of realities—the legal reality on one hand and the social reality governed by customary laws on the other hand. However, there can be no two interpretations of gender equality. Gender equality has to be viewed in a holistic perspective—it includes social, economic and political empowerment as well. One kind of empowerment cannot be viewed in isolation from the other. Right to political, economic and social opportunities irrespective of sex is enshrined in the country's constitution as well as being an integral part of the United Nations Declaration of Human Rights (UNDHR). One arena which is of serious concern to the Naga society today is on the issue of women's political rights. In this context, claims of Naga society as a 'pure democracy' as put forward by many scholars can be argued to be mere fallacy. When women who constitute approximately fifty per cent of our society are denied the chance to voice their views and opinions in decision-making bodies, where does the question of democracy, equality, justice and human rights come in? True, Naga women did not have to fight for the right to vote. But, political equality includes not only the right to franchise but also the more important right to gain access to formal institutionalized centres of power. And that is precisely the problem faced by Naga women today. For centuries, they have been excluded from institutions of decision-making. And if one look at the society today, in spite of the apparent sense of modernization especially in the urban areas women are missing where it matters the most—political institutions, both

* Ao, Temsula

traditional and modern. Nagas may take pride on claims of being an egalitarian society but the deliberate and structural exclusion of women from decision making bodies is the most damning illustration of societal discrimination against women in Naga society. Naga women are today fighting for rights to be recognized as persons, an individual, to fully grow and develop her potentials. Recognition of this right would be the first giant step towards gender equality and distributive justice in Naga society.

The present book seeks to delve into the challenges encountered by Naga women in their quest for political empowerment. The broader aim of the book is to understand the social dynamics at play in their social and cultural setting which impacts upon their political participation in particular and their social status in general. Gender issues and related problems are some of the most talked about issues today. Yet, in Nagaland, no systematic study has been carried out from a sociological perspective on this very important issue. The scarcity of systematic research thus leaves a gap to be bridged. This work is, therefore, an attempt to fill the gap by adding some insight to the Sociology of Gender in the tribal context in general and in the Naga context in particular. As there was no established literature on Naga women's participation in politics, the book sourced entirely from primary data from the field and election records. As an empirical piece of work a representative sample of five hundred women from all sections of society cutting across professions, tribes, age, marital status and educational qualifications were selected through purposive random sampling method. Due care was taken to have proportionate representation from both rural and urban areas. The conclusion arrived at were based on an examination of the electoral participation of the Naga women in terms of voting, contesting in elections, being members of political parties and campaigning during elections. It was carried out through an analysis of data garnered from the field, and an analysis of the records of the General State Assembly Elections of Nagaland held from 1964 up to 2003. Since field work for the present book was conducted another General Assembly Election was held in 2008 but the outcome and conclusion remains the same, as, even though four women contested in the said election, none of them were elected. The analysis was limited to the State Assembly Elections, whilst the Lok Sabha Elections have been purposefully excluded from the purview of the present analysis because Naga people in general accord more importance to the State Assembly Elections on the ground that the policies and programmes of the State legislatures directly affect them. On the other hand, once the elections to the Lok Sabha are held, the lone member from the State to the Upper House of Parliament hardly makes an impact on the day-to-day life of the people in the State. Thus, from a contextual perspective the elections to the State Legislature were far more important to the people of the State. The research technique employed was a combination of structured questionnaire, personal interviews, as well as group discussions. The findings provide invaluable insights into the pattern of women's political participation in the State as well as the value Naga society places in this arena of female activity against the backdrop of gender relations and the question of gender equity in the society at large.

Toshimenla Jamir

Acknowledgements

This book would not have become a reality without the unvarying support and encouragement of my husband Dr. Lanusashi, who has been the motivating force as well as the chief critic, urging me onward with his insightful constructive criticisms towards this end. My heartfelt gratitude goes to Prof. A. Lanu Ao, Dean of the School of Social Sciences, Nagaland University, for his invaluable suggestions during the course of this work. Special thanks to Dr. Xonzoi Barbora for painstakingly going through the manuscript in record time. I remain grateful to Mrs. Sano Vamuzo, the Chairperson of Nagaland State Women Commission for writing the thoughtful foreword to the book.

To my mother and father Tiala Aonok and Kati Jamir, I thank you for never underrating me for being a woman, despite societal pressure.

February 2011 **Toshimenla Jamir**

Contents

Abbreviations

AICC	All India Congress Committee
ALP	Australian Labour Party
AWPO	Angami Women Public Organization
BJP	Bharatiya Janata Party
CEDAW	Convention on the Elimination of all forms of Discrimination Against Women
CSWI	Committee on the Status of Women in India
DAW	Division for Advancement of Women
ESCAP	Economic and Social Commission for Asia and Pacific
ENWO	Eastern Naga Women's Organization
GAD	Gender and Development
GB	Gaon Bura
IPU	Inter-Parliamentary Union
ILO	International Labour Organization
INC	Indian National Congress
NMA	Naga Mother's Association
NWH	Naga Women Hoho
NBCC	Nagaland Baptist Council of Churches
NWU	Naga Women's Union
NPF	Naga People's Front
NNDP	Naga National Democratic Party
NPCC	Nagaland Pradesh Congress Committee

NDM	National Democratic Movement
OSAGI	Office of the Special Advisor on Gender Issues and Advancement of Women
STH	Sumi Totimi Hoho
UDHR	Universal Declaration of Human Rights
UNESCO	United Nations Educational, Social and Cultural Organization
VDB	Village Development Board

1
Introduction

Discourses on tribal women, of which there are not many, invariably throw up contrasting pictures. In 1978, the Indian Anthropological Society brought out a region-wise survey of tribal women which points out that except in some works by Elwin Verrier, Haimendorf and a few others, there has been no explicit discussion on the 'status of women' in tribal society.[1] Even in these, while the assessment of the status of women is far from uniform, generally women in tribal societies are portrayed as enjoying a better social position than their counterparts in other parts of the country. Concern for a focus on women in tribal societies fuelled by the emergent interest with women's issues the world over is very recent. Today, developments and change in tribal societies, particularly the change in the mode of living reflected in the change from swidden (*jhum*) to settled agriculture and the subsequent shift from communal and collective ownership of land to private ownership have led to a critical examination of the idea of tribal society as an egalitarian one. Emerging studies show that of all the forms of inequality in tribal society in its traditional setting, gender inequality is perceived as being most pervasive.[2] Naga society is no exception. Like many other tribal societies, the Nagas have a patriarchal social structure that is characterized by the notion of male superiority. Traditional and cultural impediments work against women's equal access to power. Women in Naga society suffer from multiple barriers which bar them from active political involvement. The unbalanced gender relations in tribal societies like the Nagas is made possible by a rigid dichotomy between the private and the public spheres represented by home and the domestic affairs in the former, and the outside world of governance and decision-making in the latter.

In general, gender as a social construct gives rise to stereotype formulations which severely restricts the social roles of women. The United Nations International Decade for Women has led to a growing intellectual interest in gender issues and has indeed legitimated the investigation of women as a distinct social category. Subsequent studies have documented how gender inequities persist across class, religion, cultural and other ethnic lines and how they vary in form and intensity. Women obviously are not a homogeneous group because they vary in terms of social class, ethnicity, religious affiliations, etc. Consequently, they face a variety of conditions peculiar to their own societies. Correspondingly, there is also undeniably a commonality of experiences and interests among women. Similar sexual issues tend to be faced by women regardless of social class and wealth. Above all, although social roles of women have been changing through the ages, women's status is still made to depend primarily on the biological fact that she is potentially the bearer of children. Undoubtedly, the reproductive role of women has created conditions resulting in their lagging behind men which was further legitimized over the ages through customs and legislations. The cumulative effect of this entire process is gender subordination. Gender inequality is a ubiquitous phenomenon. In 1945, the United Nations (UN) Charter proclaimed equality between men and women. Again in 1948, the Universal Declaration of human Rights (UDHR) reaffirmed the belief in the equal rights of men and women, first laid down by the nations of the world in the Charter of the United Nations. However, it is clear today that progress towards equality for women in most parts of the world is considerably less than what has been promised. The United Nations Development Programme (UNDP) Human Development Report comments that in no society are women secure or treated as equal to men. Personal insecurity shadows them from cradle to grave on account of their gender.

The concept of 'Gender' has attracted a significant amount of scholarly attention. Although 'gender' has already been used as a grammatical term, it was adopted by the feminist scholars in the 1970s to describe and analyze sexual difference. As early as 1960, Simone de Beauvoir wrote: "One is not born, but rather becomes a woman".[3] Such feminist literature advocates that 'Gender' is a cultural construct in a patriarchal society. Beauvoir drew upon a whole range of philosophical, psychological, anthropological, historical, literary and anecdotal material to argue that the most important obstacle to a woman's freedom was not her biology, or the political and legal constraints placed upon her or even her economic situation, rather it was the whole process by which femininity is manufactured in society.

Gender has also been defined as "The qualitative and interdependent character of women and men in society".[4] It is constituted in terms of the relation of power and dominance that structure the life chances of women and men. Very often the terms 'sex' and 'gender' are used interchangeably. However feminist insists that there is a clear distinction between these two terms. Accordingly, while the term 'sex' is equated with the biological characteristics of males and females, 'gender' on the other hand refers to the socially produced attributes of masculinity and femininity and the social arrangements based upon them. Thus gender, although based on biological difference, are socially and culturally created (Susan Bullock, 1994).

OSAGI (Office of the Special Advisor on Gender Issues and Advancement of Women) defines the concept of 'Gender' as, the social attributes and opportunities associated with being male and female and the relationships between women and men and girls and boys, as well as the relations between women and those between men. These attributes, opportunities and relationships are socially constructed and are learned through socialization processes. They are context and time specific and, therefore, changeable. Gender determines what is expected, allowed and valued in a woman or a man in a given context. In most societies there are differences and inequalities between women and men in responsibilities assigned, activities undertaken, access to and control over resources, as well as decision-making opportunities.[5] Gender division is, hence, not biologically fixed but constitutes an aspect of the wider social division of labour, which in turn is rooted in the condition of production and reproduction, reinforced by the cultural, production and ideological systems prevailing in society. Subsequently, in most societies, significant gender gaps in prospects and earnings remain and all national work forces continue to be highly segregated along the gender lines.

The social construction of gender, i.e., what constitutes masculine qualities and what constitutes feminine qualities can be deemed to be a system of power that assigns greater value to the activities associated with masculinity. To deem as natural or inborn the qualities or values that are actually socially and culturally constructed, is a very effective strategy for keeping the present balance of power between men and women in society. When women believe that differences in status are part of the 'natural order of things', they are less likely to challenge how differences are organized to benefit men more than women. The concept of Gender occupies centre stage in feminist theories, which argue that no phenomenon can be properly understood without a consideration of gender. Taylor and Miller (1990) opine that gender organizes social life, social structure and social beliefs. Gender theories point out how cultural restrictions contribute to the establishment of what is acceptable work for women through an extreme form of stereotyping. For instance, according to Carretson (1974), a woman who is too closely associated with her job, too successful, or too dedicated, is often labelled 'masculine'. She cites studies by Komarosky (1946), Bernard (1971) and Horner (1972), all of whom found that the hesitation shown by many women to flout this cultural prescription has been seen as the motive to avoid success. The aggressive, and by implication, masculine qualities inherent in a capacity for mastering intellectual problems, attacking difficulties, and making final decisions are considered fundamentally antagonistic to or incompatible with femininity. Garretson concludes that a woman can play a supportive role in which she chooses not to use her capabilities to the fullest extent, so that her achievements will not equal those of a man and will not threaten his dominance or her vision of her 'femininity'.

The socio-cultural system that systematically excludes women from the mainstream, keeping them less capable and denying them equal opportunities is shaped and strengthened by the values embodied in patriarchy. In most societies, the patriarchal social structure provides the ideal setting for the operation of gender and related norms. Generally 'patriarchy' is used to refer to male domination in power relationship with women. Walby (1995) defines patriarchy as "a system of social structures and practices in which men dominate, oppress and exploit women". An important factor that has contributed to the perpetuation of patriarchal norms is because women have for millennia participated in the process of their own subordination for they have been psychologically shaped so as to internalize the idea of their inferiority[6]. According to a report of the International Labour Organization (ILO), women and girls constitute one-half of the world's population and one-third of the official labour force and perform nearly two-thirds of work hours, they receive only one-tenth of the world's income and less than one-hundredth of the world's property.[7] The publication of this report by the ILO caught the world's attention and brought the seriousness of the problem to the fore. There is widespread agreement about the fact that women are all but excluded from access to and control over national and international resources, and about the resulting damage to human dignity. As late as the 1960s the development establishments not only paid little attention to the significance of the sexual division of labour, but also avoided facing the issues of class differences among groups of people. They relied on the assumption that the benefits of development would gradually trickle down to the lower classes. However, a pioneering study by Boserup[8] refutes such belief. She points out how colonialism and the attendant forms of modernization lowered women's status while raising the social status of men, by imposing new patterns of gender roles in farming and trading, and by carrying such inequalities to the new industrial and urban sectors.

During the seventies, the women's movement highlighted the marginalization of women in the economy through the Women in Development (WID) approach. Hence, the WID approach seeks to recognize and integrate women in aid policies and programmes of most development agencies. In the eighties, women's groups made an effort to integrate women in the economy. But the control of men over the means of production, exchange and distribution allowed women very limited space to evolve a development alternative with women. The decade of the nineties is marked by an approach of Gender and Development (GAD). Here the focus is on the power relations determined as a result of the interplay of complex class, caste, ethnicity, religion, race and gender.[9] The basic themes set up by the United Nations for the International Decade for Women (1975-1985) was Equality, Development and Peace, which remain the guiding points for the subsequent World Conferences on Women—The Mexico Conference 1975, The Copenhagen Conference 1980, The Nairobi Conference 1985, and the Beijing Conference 1995. The Action Plans drawn up after the World Conferences touched upon every aspect of women's lives in order to promote positive and definitive actions both at the national and international levels, in areas of education, health, nutrition, family planning, population, political participation, and employment. Subsequent to the fourth World Conference on Women held at Beijing in 1995, the Beijing 'Platform for action' recognized the gender gaps in economic power, property rights and poverty. It also clearly connects women's poverty and gender inequality. Women's poverty is directly related to the absence of economic opportunities and autonomy, lack of access to economic resources, including credit, land ownership and inheritance, education, and support services, and minimal participation at the decision-making process.[10] Further, the Platform also recognizes the link between the economic and the political, that the eradication of poverty cannot be accomplished through anti-poverty programmes alone, but will require democratic participation and changes in economic resources, opportunities and public services.

REFERENCES

1. Xaxa, Virginius, "Women and Gender in the Study of Tribes in India", *Indian Journal of Gender Studies*, Vol. 11, No. 3, New Delhi, Sage Publications, 2004.
2. *Ibid.*
3. Beauvoir, Simone de, *The Second Sex* (Harmondsworth: Penguin, 1972).

4. Ostergaard, Lise, (ed.), *Gender and Development: A Practical Guide,* (London: Routledge Publication, 1992).
5. 'Mainstreaming Gender' (http://www.un.org/womenwatch/osagi/gender/mainstreaming.htm).
6. Lerner, Gerda, *The Creation of Patriarchy* (New York: Oxford University Press, 1986).
7. Jahan, R., *The Elusive Agenda: Mainstreaming Women and Development,* 1996.
8. Boserup, E., *Women's Role in Economic Development,* (London: George and Unwin, 1970).
9. Patel, Vibhuti, *Women's Challenges of the New Millennium,* (New Delhi: Gyan Publishing House, 2002).
10. Agarwal, Bina; "From Mexico to Beijing", 1995, *Indian Journal of Gender Studies,* 3:1, New Delhi, 1996, p. 91.

2
Women and Political Participation

Women are still underrepresented in politics virtually in all parts of the world, with the exception of a few countries. Women face even more barriers and resistance to enter politics in traditional and conservative societies that have a limited view of women's roles in public life. Some four decades ago, more emphasis was stressed on economics as a path for women to attain greater equity, today realization has dawned on policy makers and activists all over the globe that political empowerment is the key towards distributive justice and gender equity in all sense. Hence, current emphasis has been shifted to politics—local, national and global. Women's struggle today covers a wide spectrum of issues, and activists within the women's movement believe that women's participation in the political process is not only central to the functioning and strengthening of democracy but equally crucial to their struggle against oppression and their ability to challenge the ideologies and hierarchies which keep them subordinate.[1] It was the theory of classical liberalists of the eighteenth century who analyzed political participation as a 'Natural Right' instrumental in resisting all kinds of despotism. Women's political participation is becoming a central issue in present time against the unfolding realities of oppression and subjugation tacitly sanctioned by customary norms and values. Almond and Verba (1963)[2] opined that as roles became specialized and persons became oriented to the inputs and outputs of the government, a participant political culture was seen as growing out of economic and social development. There cannot be a meaningful democracy or true people's participation in governance and development without equal participation of women and men in all spheres of life and at different levels of decision-making. Besides, any goals of development cannot be realized without women's full and active participation not only in development process but also in the shaping of its goals.[3] Political participation and the subsequent empowerment of women assume great significance within this context. Political empowerment through participation is envisaged as an aid to help women achieve equality with men, or, at least reduce the gender gap considerably.

A Democracy is a political system in which the opportunity to participate in decision-making is widely shared among all adult citizens.[4] Democracy depends on an informed and engaged citizenry, one that acquires the knowledge and skills needed to become politically involved and then participates actively. Therefore, in a participatory democracy, political participation becomes a basic necessity and the principal means by which a political system generates legitimacy and maintains stability.[5] The concept of political participation is very broad. In general political participation is understood as involvement in politics. Politics, according to David Easton, is the process of 'authoritative allocation of values' for the society, and political participation refers to popular attempts or activities designed to influence this 'allocation of values'. It is the conscious, deliberate participation in the political process by which resources are allocated amongst people. Similarly, in a UNESCO seminar held at Lisbon, the participants defined the sphere of politics which includes 'the social relations that create and institutionalize power relations and use them to foster control and manipulate people's behaviour, attitudes and beliefs in order to supervise and regulate the distribution of resource'.[6]

It is generally agreed that political power is a key to gaining control over the community's resources. Political participation is a means of gaining access to the power-structure where decisions with regard to the allocation of resources amongst people and other issues of the community's concern are made. Political participation involves articulating, providing and defending interests. Elections can provide the best possible opportunity to ensure women's voices are heard, their concerns are addressed, and their potential contributions to peace and democracy are maximized. Electoral rights means much more than simply the right to vote. Political participation has taken a variety of forms in different democracies and this has gradually extended the scope of the concept beyond voting. Political participation derives from the freedom to speak out, assemble and associate, the ability to take part in the conduct of public affairs, and the opportunity to register as a candidate, to campaign, to be elected and hold office at all levels of government. It is generally accepted that participation also implies activities in the period between elections when citizens try to influence Government decisions. This view is reflected in the definition given by Mathew and Prothos which says that "Political participation includes all behaviour through which people directly express their opinion".[7] In this sense, political participation includes a whole range of activities such as taking part in political campaigns, strikes, petitioning, demonstrations, political membership, discussing politics, contesting in elections, besides exercising one's franchise. Freedom of expression, assembly and association, and the freedom to take part in the conduct of public affairs, hold public office at all levels of government, and participate in the formulation of government policy are, therefore, all subsumed under this heading. The Inter-Parliamentary Union (IPU) holds that democracy will assume true significance only when political policies and legislation are decided jointly by men and women in the interests of both halves of the population—a partnership for democracy.[8]

An understanding of the political system creates awareness and interest in politics.[9] Political consciousness or awareness would thus refer to actual knowledge of a person about public events and political affairs. Education is often regarded as the most important factor that widens the scope of one's acquaintance with political facts, to increase capacity to perceive the personal implication of political events. Political consciousness can be an awareness about political parties and functioning of the government, social and developmental issues, political developments, and also awareness about women's rights and deprivations. The absence or invisibility of women in politics does not suggest gender neutrality but in fact demonstrates the personal, political, systematic and structural effects of gender differentiation.

To recognize this structural differentiation between the sexes is essentially a political task by the women. Hence, this awakening can be equated to political consciousness.

The theme of political participation and political status of women has generated considerable debate. Political status of women is the degree of equality and freedom enjoyed by women in the shaping and sharing of power and in the value given by society to this role of women.[10] This equality is inseparable from the active political participation of women in political life and is integral to the advancement of women. Women in general have steadily increased their responsibilities as voters but they have not yet assumed significant responsibility at the governance of State. And where they have, their number has been small. The point is well illustrated in a document of the United Nations entitled 'Women At A Glance'.[11] According to this document, only 24 women have been elected heads of State or governments in this century; women hold only 10.5 per cent of the seats in the world's parliaments; of the highest-ranking diplomats to the United Nations, only seven are women. The above facts indicate that in regard to political and governing power, in no case do women share equally in the political participation of a State. The New Delhi Document on Women in Development 1985 recognized that despite the rapid growth of informal political activity by women, their role in the growth of formal structure had virtually remained unchanged. This recognition has resulted in a serious debate on the concepts and indicators for political participation. Within the women's movement activists are concerned with women's under-representation in politics supported by the argument that the legal and social disabilities of women cannot be resolved without effective participation in formal political institutions. It is recognized that in order to transform the standards and agendas of politics and governance which remain male-dominated, increased women's participation in political decision-making is a desirable goal.[12]

Though political participation is a given right in any democracy, the participation of women in most societies falls far short of men. According to The National Committee on the Status of Women in India (CSWI) report entitled 'Towards Equality' (1975) though women constituted a numerical majority, they were acquiring the features of a minority because of inequality of status and political power. The report also expressed concern over the difficulties experienced by women in obtaining adequate representation for their cause in legislative bodies. It stressed the need for improving the political status of women as an integral aspect of the political elite structure.

Political participation of women varies in relation to four major factors, i.e., (i) the extent a woman receives political stimuli, (ii) her personal characteristics, (iii) her social characteristics, and (iv) the political environment in which she finds herself. A woman's knowledge, values and attitudes, her experiences and personality affect her response to political stimuli and thus the extent to which she engages in political activity.[13] The process of political socialization provides the woman with a perpetual screen through which she receives political stimuli.[14] As a result of this, women involve themselves at various levels in the political system and in the process of political participation.

Politics typically depicts a masculine face—masculinism pervades politics. Wendy Brown writes: "More than any other kind of human activity, politics has historically borne an explicit masculine identity. It has been more exclusively limited to men than any other realm of endeavour and has been more intensely self-consciously masculine than most other social practices".[15] As such, political women are seen by some men as trespassers in a terrain which functionally belongs to men.[16] But unless women become politically visible in the national legislatures, issues that concern them would continue to receive marginal attention. Logically it is expected that women are more aware of their own needs and are, therefore, better able to press for them. Issues such as child care, women's health, reproductive rights, sexual harassment, equal employment benefits, discriminatory laws and practices against women, violence against women and other family issues derive more attention from women legislators, as exemplified from studies in Finland and the USA.[17]

Though in most nations of the world women are equal before the law and have equal opportunity to participate, their participation is likely to remain poor until efforts are made to ensure their inclusion.[18] It is to be observed as a general phenomenon that as political decision-making power increases, women's presence decreases.[19] This may happen for a variety of reasons such as general perception of politics as a male dominated activity, women's reluctance to put themselves forward, women's commitment to raise children, lack of confidence, lack of support from the husband, partner or the family, lack of financial resources to enter politics, physical strain of balancing a family, a job, and a political career. Kaushik[20] argues that marginalization of women in politics is due to women's secondary place in society. The position of women was analyzed a number of years ago in a United Nations study edited by Maurice Duverger. He too notes that the small part played by women in politics merely reflects and results from the secondary place to which they are assigned by the customs and attitudes of society and which their education tend to make them accept as the natural order of things.

A popularly held belief is that the child bearing and rearing role of women is a major factor which inhibits women from playing an active public role. This argument is reflected in the writings of Dana Raphael, who writes: "The women who have become political figures in their own right have done so after their reproductive years are over.... Apparently human beings did not find it economically feasible until recently for people in any culture to train both males and females to assume power roles and child-rearing roles".[21] Age, hence, have an important bearing on the political participation of women primarily because of her biological function of child-bearing and rearing.

Many consider women's under representation as a reflection of existing unequal sexual division of labour for it seeks to perpetuate the functionalist view of gender whereby women are perceived to be primarily mothers and home makers. This view is not only pre-modern but also pre-democratic.[22] Increasing participation of women in political process is one of the major ways in which the traditional and dominant value system can be challenged.[23] When women comprise half the potential talent and ability of humanity, their under-representation is a loss for humanity as a whole. A balanced participation by both women and men in decision-making would produce different ideas, values and styles of behaviour suited for a fairer and more balanced world for all. There is a need for political participation by women, in order to associate with political bodies so that not only pro-women policies for developmental projects are taken, but to have the right to influence such decision-making. Female political participation is a means to the ultimate goals of equality and true democratic representation. The Human Development Report 1995 indicated that human development, if not engendered, is endangered.

The concern of the United Nations and women's movements throughout the world on the issue has been expressed in several fora. The Mexico World Plan of Action (1975) pointed out to the difference in political status of men and women and asked for equal access of women and men to decision-making levels in the governments. It stressed that greater and equal participation of women at all levels of decision-making would decisively contribute to accelerating the pace of development and the maintenance of peace. The World Conference on Women reiterated that women's active participation at decision-making levels was a pre-requirement to the full exercise of equal rights.

Political parties play a significant role in determining the prospect of women's political participation. Generally parties determine which candidates are nominated and elected and which issues achieve national importance. Due to the fact that political parties are so influential in shaping women's political prospects, governments and international organizations seeking to advance the participation of women in politics justifiably tend to focus on the role of political parties.

Hence, the systematic and structural inequalities between men and women are relevant to politics because democracy requires parity of representation and there cannot be meaningfully democracy if women are virtually excluded from positions of power, intentionally or otherwise. The validity of an all-male decision-making continue to be questionable in a democratic system because the very essence and principles of democracy remains unfulfilled and it cannot claim to be representative of all sections of the people when the female perspective is not taken into account. Further, equitable resource allocation cannot be expected without the participation of women in representative numbers. Thus, gender equality is a prerequisite for effective participation of women in strengthening the institutionalized structure of democracy.

The Nagas, with their rigid patriarchal social structure characterized by notions of male superiority over females, exemplifies a society with a modern facade but underpinned by deep traditional values that severely marginalizes women from institutions of decision making, both old and new. The political status of the Naga women is inextricably linked to and determined by the prevalent patriarchal socio-cultural values and ethos of their society. Women in Naga society have for millennia contributed immensely to society, quietly rendering their service albeit without any voice as a social category in the policies that impacts upon them equally as citizens. Traditional inequalities, such as unequal treatment of women in sexiest societies, often survive by making the respective identities, which may include subservient roles of the traditional underdog, matters for unquestioning acceptance, rather than reflective examination. But the unquestioned presumptions are merely unquestioned—not unquestionable.[24] It has, therefore, become imperative to critically re-evaluate the traditional social and political system where the Naga women have been simply passive takers of policy for centuries, vis-à-vis their political participation against the larger question of gender equity and empowerment of women in Naga society.

REFERENCES

1. Sharma, Kumud, "Transformative Politics: Dimensions of Women's Participation in Panchayati Raj," *Indian Journal of Gender Studies*, 5:1, Sage Publications, New Delhi, 1998, p. 23.
2. Almond,G., Sidney Verba, *The Civic Culture* (Princeton: Princeton University Press, 1963).
3. Thakur, Rashmi, "Women and Political Empowerment", *Employment News*, June 24-30, 2000, pp. 1-3.
4. Dahl, Robert A, *Modern Political Analysis*, New Delhi, 1997, p. 6
5. Tripathy, Swarnamayee, *Political Participation of Women Workers in Orissa*; New Delhi, 2000, p. 1.
6. Sharma, Kumud, no. 9.
7. Mathew, D.R and J.W. Prothos, *Negroes and the New Southern Politics*, 1966, p. 37.

8. Joseph, John, Inter-parliamentary specialized Conference on "Towards Partnership Between Men and Women in Politics", *The Journal of Parliamentary Information*, March 1997, New Delhi.
9. Tripathy, Swarnamayee; No. 5, p. 139.
10. Pujari, Premlata, V.K. Kaushik, *Women in India*, New Delhi, 1994, p. 13.
11. United Nations Department of Public Information, UN, New York, February 1997.
12. Sharma, Kumud, no. 9, p. 26.
13. Milbrath, L., *Political Participation: How and Why People Get Involved in Politics*? (Chicago: Rand McNally & CO., 1965).
14. Rush, M., Althoff, P., *An Introduction to Political Sociology* (London: Nelson, 1971).
15. Soin, Kanwaljit, *Why Women, What Politics*, Centre for Asia-Pacific Women in Politics, p. 1 (http://www.capwip.org/resources/soin/soinpaper.html), accessed on 9th June 2005.
16. Bhatt, Shanta, *Women Parliamentarians of India*, Udaipur: Shiva Publishers Distributors, 1995.
17. Soin, Kanwaljit, no. 8, p. 3.
18. Gariyali, C.K., *Inching Forward: Political Empowerment of Women in Commonwealth Countries*, New Delhi: Vitri Publishers, 1999.
19. Rajland, Beatiz in *Women and Globalization*, edited by Rajput and Swarup, New Delhi, 1994, p. 145.
20. Kaushik, Susheela, (ed.), *Women's Oppression, Patterns and Perspectives*, New Delhi: Shakti Books, 1985.
21. Raphael, Dana (ed.); *Being Female: Reproduction, Power and Change*, Hague, 1975, p. 3.
22. Ramaswamy, Sushila, *Women's Human Rights: A Global Perspective*, Nagaland, Post 23 June, 2000.
23. Giri, V. Mohini, *Emancipation and Empowerment of Women*, New Delhi: Gyan Publishing House, 1998.
24. Sen, Amartya, *Reason before Identity*, Oxford University Press, 1999, p. 19.

3

Naga Women in Social Setting

Naga women's experience as a woman is embedded in her particular culture. Political participation is invariably influenced and determined to a great extent by the socio-cultural environment of a given society. It is the culture of a society that incites not only action but also provides information about boundaries and barriers that conditions the individual to choose among alternative courses of action. For instance, though everybody gets more or less equal exposure to media during elections, the degree of participation differs from person to person. This can be accounted for by the fact that social circumstances and cultural factors play a crucial role either in facilitating or depriving individuals from exerting control over their destiny, an attitude clearly compatible with the belief that environmental conditions determines the individual's behaviour. Being a traditional society deep rooted in their culture, an analysis of the political participation of Naga women need to delve into their cultural setting in order to understand the dynamics of their political behaviour, because every facet of the life of a Naga, be it religious, social or political, are based on tradition and culture.

A Brief Profile of Naga Social Structure

Nagaland is a small State nestled in the North-Eastern corner of India, bordered on the west by Assam, on the North-East by Arunachal

Pradesh, in the South by Manipur and by Myanmar on the East. There are sixteen officially recognized Naga tribes in the State namely: Ao, Angami, Chang, Chakhesang, Konyak, Khiamniungan, Kuki, Lotha, Phom, Pochury, Rengma, Sangtam, Sema, Tikhir, Yimchungru, Zeliang, and some other minor tribes. No Naga tribe has any written record of their early history, and so traditions and customs are passed on orally from generation to generation, through the medium of folklores, songs, and legends. The Nagas as a whole exhibit a rich traditional heritage and has a similar culture and much in common in their way of life and customs. Being basically an agriculturist society, Naga women in general have always been co-workers along men in traditional agriculture. Women, particularly in rural areas, contribute substantially towards the process of food production and they carry major responsibility in procuring and preparing food for family consumption. At the same time there are certain distinct characteristics that differentiate the culture of one Naga tribe from the other. In Naga society, the village, not the tribe, is the primary political and social unit. Every Naga village was very much a world unto itself. Without exception, all the Naga tribes practise clan exogamy. An erstwhile common feature of the Naga tribes was head-hunting, which formed a significant aspect in the social life of the Nagas. This practice was stopped through the combined efforts of the forces of British colonial rule and the American missionaries.

A common trait of most tribal societies can be found in division of labour which is based more on gender and age than on hierarchy and occupation. An important traditional institution found in many Naga tribes was the institution of Bachelors' dormitory commonly known as *Morung*[1], and the Girls' dormitory known variously in different local dialects such as *Tsüki* (Ao), *Kichuki* (Angami), etc., which accommodated young boys and girls respectively on reaching puberty till the time they get married. The functions of the male and female institutions varied greatly. In the past, there was no tribal or inter-tribal organization to deal with the needs of the tribe as a whole, so each village became solely responsible for its own economic, social, spiritual and political needs.[2] Such needs required that the young be taught and trained within the village community. Accordingly, the most important training institutions in Naga society were the youth dormitories. As stated earlier, much of the Naga culture, its customs and traditions have been transmitted orally from generation to generation through the medium of folklores, folk music and dance, folk tales and oral traditions, besides designs on clothes. Much of the teaching-learning processes evolved from these traditional institutions. The *Morung* further had a protective and disciplinary function for the boys. Naga villages in the days of yore were characterized by frequent raids and inter-village wars. Hence, the villagers were always in fear of a war and it was necessary to have a disciplined band of young warriors ready for any emergency. The Morung thus functioned as a guardhouse to warn the villagers in times of war. It also served as a recreational club for the youth of the village.

Evidently the *Morung* played a more pivotal role in the village polity as against the *Tsüki*, as portrayed through an account of their functions. The primary reason for its relative importance derived from the fact that besides the obvious social functions performed by this institution, it also served as the centre of most policy decision-making in the village. Every strategic policy formulation such as for the defence of the village, or offensive strategies against other villages for raids, development of the village—in a nutshell, most political decisions were taken at the *Morung*. The *Tsüki*, on the other hand, remained, for all purposes, merely a socio-cultural training institution. The girls were encultured to believe that they are solely responsible for housework which includes washing, cleaning, cooking, looking after children, collecting firewood, collecting water, kitchen gardening, caring for the sick at home, etc. Once its inmates matured and get married, they leave the dormitory and were inevitably consigned to the domestic drudgeries of everyday life. On the other hand, the 'graduates' of the *Morung* go on into higher seats of Village administration, like the Council of elders commonly known as the Village Council. Thus, the traditional institution for males and females in Naga society socialized their respective inmates based on a strict sexual division of labour. This point to an obvious lack of political socialization of the Naga girls in their traditional institution of learning such as the *Tsüki* which is indicative of the marginal role they are assigned to in the political sphere of the Naga polity and one that sees little change till date.

The traditional practice of 'age-group' or 'peer-group' among all the Naga tribes is a distinctive feature of the Naga socio-cultural life which prevails to date particularly in the rural areas though facets of it may also be found in the towns and cities albeit on a lesser scale. Normally, membership in an age group extended to all persons, irrespective of sex, who were born within a range of three years period. This unique traditional system of age-groups in Naga society was prevalent more significantly among those tribes who followed the practice of *Morung* System. Accordingly, one found a number of well-organized age-groups in every Naga village where dormitory system was prevalent. Each age-group had their assigned duties and responsibilities in the village. Members of an age-group could participate collectively in any festival and manual works arranged by their peers. Besides, the age-group also functioned as a support system for its members as they looked out after the welfare of each member in times of need or ill fortune. Among the Lotha Nagas for instance, on the marriage of one of its members, the age-group would construct a house for the newly married couple and store one year's supply of paddy for the couple to utilize till they can harvest their first yield of crops. Or, among the Ao Nagas, if a member of a particular age-group was unable to harvest his field due to certain unavoidable circumstances like ill health, fellow age-group members would pitch in to harvest his field as per the norms of the age-group system. The practice of 'age-grouping', hence, was a very unique practice which played a distinctive and significant function in Naga society.

Besides the common features found among every Naga tribe, there also existed specific cultural, social, and political systems particular to each tribe. For instance, with regard to the political system, there exists the chieftainship and autocratic rule among the Konyaks and Semas, whereas the Aos have a kind of republican system with Village Councils constituted of representatives from each clan in the village. There also exists the democracy of the Angamis where the quest for consensus is the norm and any citizen of the village can literally do what he likes, even go against the decision of the whole village, provided he is willing to pay the price of social stigma and ostracism. There are also variations in physical type, dress, habits and most importantly, differences in dialects among the different Naga tribes and sub-tribes.

Formal education in the modern sense was first introduced into the Naga Hills by American Baptist Missionaries in late nineteenth century, followed by the British. The first Mission was set up in 1840 by Mr. Bronson at Namsang in the Tirap frontier Division.[3] The missionaries who made a landmark in the civilization of the Nagas were Godhula Brown and Rev. E.W. Clark and his wife Mary Clark, who established church in the Ao area of the Naga Hills in 1872. Pioneering effort in education for girls among the Nagas was initially made by Mary Mead Clark, who served among the Ao Nagas for thirty-five years (1876-1911) as a woman missionary. The first formal school in the Naga Hills was started in 1878 at Molungyimsen Village by Mrs. Mary Mead Clark.[4] It was, as a matter of fact, originally intended for girls. The purpose of educating the Naga girls by the Missionaries was so that the Naga converts can have Christian wives who can build Christian homes. Therefore, the initial objective for the girls' education in Nagaland by the western missionaries was not so much for its own sake, but with the agenda of proselytizing the Christian faith. However, it was not a task easily achieved. Ethel May Stevenson, the Head of the girls' school at Impur in Mokokchung district of Nagaland reported in 1917 that it was still very difficult to persuade Naga parents to send their daughters for schooling.[5] The chief concern of the parents was that there would be no one to do the domestic chores in the house, as well as farm work if their daughters were to be sent to school, pointing to the almost regimented gender division of labour that existed in Naga society. However, despite the initial hesitation and qualms of the Nagas with regard to education for girls, the efforts of the Christian Missionaries paid off and the literacy rate of Naga women stands today at 76.67 per cent against the total State literacy rate of 80.11 per cent (2011 Census).

Table 3.1: Total Population and Literate Population by Sex of Nagaland (2011 Census)

Total Population	Literate Population		
	Persons	Male	Female
1,980,602	1,357,579 80.11%	731,796 83.29%	625,783 76.69%

Source: Census of India 2011, Nagaland, Series 14.

Though the literacy rate of the women in Nagaland falls short of men which stand at 83.29 per cent, it is much higher than the all India female literacy rate of 65.46 per cent (2011 Census).[6]

Modern democratic system of governance was ushered into the State with the granting of full-fledged Statehood on 1st December, 1963. Today elections are held under the banner of different national and regional political parties of the country. Yet, the framework of the village organization and the social structure are still strong and the party politics has not made deep impact on the fabric of the traditional socio-political set-up of the Naga village. Further, the customary laws and traditions of Nagas are safeguarded by a special provision under the Indian Constitution, Article 371(A), which reads:

> "Notwithstanding anything in this Constitution—
> No Act of Parliament in respect of
> (i) Religious or social practices of the Nagas,
> (ii) Naga customary law and procedure,
> (iii) Administration of civil and criminal justice involving decisions according to Naga customary law,
> (iv) Ownership and transfer of land and its resources, shall apply to the State of Nagaland unless the Legislative Assembly of *Nagaland by a resolution so decides.*"[7]

Hence, despite the changes brought about by the modern polity and economic development, the primordial social structure of Naga society has shown little sign of fragility. The rules of the clans, customary laws and the village integrity are strongly adhered to and maintained.

Gender Relations in the Past

A review of the literature on the Nagas with reference to the position of women in society throws up puzzling contradictions in the conclusions drawn by scholars and observers with respect to the status of women in their society. Many of the Colonial administrators-cum-anthropologists who served and wrote in the

Naga Hills during the early modern period appeared to have a positive view on the status of women. J.P. Mills wrote: *"An Ao woman is very far from being a slave and drudge. Her position is no whit inferior to that of men"*.[8] Similarly, Mead Clark, a pioneer missionary, who had worked among the Ao Nagas for some twenty years, wrote: *"There is no degradation of women among this rude, uncivilized people"*.[9] M. Horam opined that the position of women in Naga society is far from secondary or subordinate. According to him, all her life a woman enjoys considerable freedom.[10] On the other hand, J.H. Hutton (1921) cites an officer named Davies who wrote that after marriage they '*became mere household drudge*'.[11] Other writings, particularly by local scholars, lean towards the latter view which sees Naga women as occupying an inferior position relative to men (Ao 1980; Talitemjen 1997; Aier 1998 and Longchar 1999).

Faced with such contradictions, the cultural life of the Nagas presents a window into the reality of women in Naga society. Clearly, the institutions of *Morung* and *Tsuki* socialized boys and girls into gender specific roles. Naga society was characterized by strict norms and attitudes of patriarchy which had a significant bearing on the status of women. Prior to the advent of Christianity, the Nagas had their own indigenous religion and were highly superstitious. They were expected to carry on their various religious duties and much of their life was lived in strict conformity with the religious law executed by the village priest who was always consulted before any important decision was taken. Traditionally, a Naga woman could not become the religious head of her family, clan or the village and was debarred from performing religious rites and sacrifices. Women were not allowed to come to the village common altar.

A woman in Naga society could not become the village chief as this was considered a breach of the divine law. The rationale behind this was that a village ruled by a woman is cursed in the sight of God as this is against his will. The priests have always said this and so the people believed it without questioning.[12] Female sexuality was believed to be impure and polluted. The Ao Nagas believed that a man has three souls and three spirits while a woman has two souls and three spirits. This difference was applicable in all the performance of ceremonies during sickness, death, birth, etc.[13] The Naga social structure is reflected by notions such as the birth of a male child being auspicious, man as a breadwinner and protector of the society, and woman being subordinate to their husbands.[14] In traditional Naga society, the status of a woman was derived in relation to her family as a daughter, wife, sister and mother. The Naga law of inheritance permits only males to inherit property. Females have no such rights. A woman in Ao Naga society suffers from disqualification in the following ways:[15]

1. She cannot become a member of *Tatar Putu Menden*.[16]
2. She cannot become a *Putir* (priest), even though she may be the oldest person in the village. Thus, she is debarred from performing religious rites and sacrifices.
3. She cannot participate in debates and discussions of public interest.
4. She cannot inherit landed property.

Further, in the Ao Naga society, even the name of a woman is returned back to her paternal clan after her death, saying something to the effect of: *The name of so or so is hereby returned back to you*. This declaration is made by her husband's clan members. Thereafter, the same name continues to be used by her internal clan members. Such cultural practice is indicative of the fact that women in Naga society are regarded akin to property. The notion of female as weaker is very much present in the Lotha society too. Males are supposed to possess six strengths, whereas the females only five. Thus males are christened on the 6th day and females on the 5th day.[17] Similarly, in Angami society, a daughter is not entitled to own any of the ancestral property. If the woman is an only child, the ancestral property will be given to her father's immediate male relatives. In matters of divorce, children born out of wedlock, sexual harassment and rape, or treatment of widows, customary laws are generally biased against women.[18]

On the whole, the secondary position of Naga women is nowhere more evident than in its traditional decision-making institutions. In Angami society for instance, when the villagers meet to make decisions, women are not allowed to voice their feelings. The male clubs where decisions are taken are taboo for women. Similar is the case among the Ao Nagas and the other Naga tribes. Traditionally, it was considered to be a 'bad omen' if a woman comes nearby the *Ariju* because that was where crucial decisions pertaining to the entire village were made. The *raison d'être* being that, women were considered as profane. Moreover, it is said, often the men folk doubted the ability of the women to maintain the confidentiality of the matters being discussed in the *Ariju*. For instance, among the Ao Naga tribe, women are not allowed to attend the *Senso Mungdang* (Annual Ao-Naga Citizens' Meeting) even to date, where all decisions pertaining to Village development, tradition, history, etc., are reviewed and deliberated for posterity. Important policy-decisions which would be binding and applicable to the entire village were also taken in such meetings. This tradition of female exclusion from important decision-making processes is to be similarly found in almost every Naga tribe.

At present the *Hoho* remains the most important traditional decision-making institution which is developed at various levels—Naga *Hoho*, different tribal *Hohos*, and the village level *Hohos*. The Naga *Hoho* represents the entire Nagas, and is considered the apex traditional decision-making body in the State, constituted by representatives from various tribes. In line with the traditional practice, no woman representatives are included in the Naga *Hoho*. At the village level, the Village Council is the apex decision-making body, which is represented by all the clans in the village. However, only a male member could represent his clan. Thus, customary laws do not allow women to be part of decision-making institutions, nor participate in public debates or meetings. Such exclusion of women from public forums serves effectively to render them politically incapable, sometimes even to the point of ignorance, even in matters that affect them such as policy decisions for development of the village and community.

Despite their marginalization from institutions of decision-making, men and women in Naga society have always worked side by side in agricultural production. *Jhum* or swidden cultivation was the traditional mode of agriculture except in some areas where terrace farming was practiced. In *jhum* cultivation, other than the clearing and burning of jungle, which was considered predominantly a male function, other functions such as sowing, weeding, harvesting, etc., were carried out mainly by the women. Therefore, they played a major role in the production process.

The customary laws which govern every aspect of Naga society including gender relations were passed on orally from generation to generation with its own formalization of behaviour, enforcement procedures, and punishment for violators.

Contemporary Social Dynamics of Naga Women

Progressive modernization brought by the adoption of Christianity, spread of modern education and introduction of democratic political system have gradually altered the contemporary situation among the Naga women. The emphasis on the education for women undertaken by the Christian Missionaries brought noteworthy changes to the lives of the Naga women. For one, it brought them out of the domestic and farming arenas. It provided opportunities for women to assume new positions of significance in new institutions like schools, offices, hospitals, etc. F.S. Downs views Christianity as the primary instrument of change in the role of women.[19] Prior to Christianity, the Nagas had their own indigenous religion, which is all but obliterated today. Christianity is today the dominant religion in Nagaland (92 per cent of total population, 2001 Census). Under the influence of Christianity, superstitions and traditional belief systems gave way to Christian faith and belief systems. Christianity played a fundamental role in eradicating the practice of head-hunting in Naga society. It can be said that Christianity and education were like two sides of the same coin which had been responsible for bringing profound changes to the social as well as economic life of the Nagas. The Christian faith brought about new attitude and a new perspective in life. The Christian faith teaches that the purpose of creation in life is based on positive principles whereby men and women are to share life with full freedom and total equality. They are to complement one another by being created uniquely different from each other. Christianity is thus essentially egalitarian in principle and seeks to accord equality, dignity and respect to women. These principles of the new faith redefined gender relations to a large extent in Naga society by creating a space for women in the deeply patriarchal social structure that had hitherto existed. This was particularly reflected in the opinion of many women with regard to the benefits of involvement in the church organizations. Many women who were involved in the church talked about realizing their self-worth through their active participation in the church. It can be inferred hence that the church provided them with a sense of self-worth and dignity which helped to enhance their perception of self in the patriarchal social set-up.

Christianity thus purportedly evoked a new outlook, a worldview, and a largely positive attitude amongst Naga women. Whereas in traditional society women had played a narrower role, their movement being confined to home, child rearing, cultivation and domestic responsibilities, in the new social order women became more mobile in their involvement in social affairs. However, this is not to say that they acquired leadership roles because under the new ecclesiastical order women were still assigned a subordinate role. They are excluded from most decision-making bodies in the church. In fact, traditional patriarchal structures resembling that of the larger society can be seen reflected in the structure of church ministry, in which women are consigned to primarily assisting roles. From the very beginning, it appears that Christianity has not encouraged women's leadership, except in the fields of education and health services.[20] Christianity to a large extent was conditioned by traditionalism of the Naga society. Even qualified and experienced women were denied of top leadership roles, such as pastoral work or to be head of the various mission fields. Women were inducted only up to the position of associate pastors. Further, the Deacon Boards of the churches which supposedly were the highest decision-making bodies within the church were overwhelmingly comprised of only male members. At present efforts are on within certain tribal communities to make it more gender inclusive.

In the immediate wake of severe economic changes that took place in Naga society when they came in contact with the outside world, particularly the monetization of the economy, distinct changes in the gender relations became visible. Many women became increasingly dependent on their husbands who assumed the role of bread winners. In the lead up to the new system of education introduced by western missionaries, men were the first to get formal education, with many parents reluctant to send their daughters to school for reasons such as elucidated earlier. These earliest educated men were, in the absence of any secondary sector, incorporated into the tertiary sector of government services. The first generation of service-men in the slowly evolving urban administrative centres and towns were married to girls who, not being educated, were almost entirely dependent on them. This saw Naga women becoming more dependent on their husbands for their subsistence which was a far cry from their earlier position of being equal co-workers in the productive arena. Their contribution to household subsistence became far more limited than it was in the past. This further accentuated the private-public divide in Naga society among the two genders.

Politically, Naga women today along with the rest of the Indian citizens enjoy the right to suffrage under the democratic framework. It is to be said, however, that socio-cultural factors play a determining role in determining the extent and nature of their political participation. Besides, women's political behaviour is associated with several background characteristics including age, marital status, religion, and educational qualification. In addition, women's status and autonomy in decision-making are critical in promoting political activity, especially in patriarchal societies like that of the Nagas. For a Naga woman, child care and domestic duties are understood to be her sole responsibilities. But, it is the husband, the 'bread-winner' of the family, who wields the ultimate authority in the family. The final decision in the house often rests with the husband. In the case of an unmarried woman in Naga society, she has to submit to the authority of her father.

Many Naga tribes had the practice of early marriage prior to Christianity. However, Table 3.2 indicates that only 1.03 per cent of males and 4.7 per cent of females among urban population and 1.06 per cent males and 2.75 per cent females in rural population get married at the age of 14-19 years. Majority of urban males (56.58%)

and females (72.67%) and rural males (37.71%) and females (51.47%) get married in the age 20-39 years.

Table 3.2: Age of Marriage (State Level)

Age at Marriage	Urban		Rural	
	Male percentage to the total Marriage population	Female percentage to the total Marriage population	Male percentage to the total Marriage population	Female percentage to the total Marriage population
Upto-14 Years	0.40	0.70	0.44	0.44
15-19 years	0.63	3.77	0.62	2.31
20-29 years	21.69	39.25	11.78	22.95
30-39 years	34.89	33.42	25.93	28.52
40-49 years	26.77	14.73	26.22	22.50
50 plus years	7.14	3.16	10.02	7.53

Source : *Gender Profile of Nagaland*, Sharma, R.C. (New Delhi: UNESCO, 2001).

Naga women today marry relatively late as compared to the all India median age of marriage which stands at 16 years.[21] In the pre-modern days early marriages in Naga society were arranged normally by the parents and relatives without proper understanding between the boy and girl being affected. This took place apparently due to the belief and practice that if either a boy or girl died before marriage, his or her name would have to be abandoned. Logically, therefore, early marriage was preferred so that if either died, their names would not be abandoned by their respective clans.[22] The fact that today more girls are opting to pursue higher education motivated by a desire to seek employment and a career leads to relatively late marriages.

An important element of contemporary Naga civil society is the presence of numerous women's groups. Almost every Naga tribe has a women's organization with the purpose of safeguarding women's rights and to remove social ills from the Naga society. Some of the women's organizations in Nagaland are the Naga Mothers Association (NMA), *Watsü Mungdang* (WM), Angami Women Public Organization

(AWPO), *Sumi Totimi Hoho* (STH), Naga Women Hoho (NWH), *Lotha Eloe Hoho*, etc. Except for the NMA and the NWH, which are not tribe-based organizations, all the other women's organizations in the State are representative of only their respective tribes and, therefore, operational in their respective districts. A recent dimension to the growth of women's organizations in the State is the emergence of regional body like the Eastern Naga Women's Organization (ENWO) which is a conglomerate representing women from the districts of Mon, Tuensang, Longleng and Kiphiri. While some of the women's organizations of Nagaland like the *Watsü Mungdang* arose primarily as socio-cultural organization with the backing of the Church, others were organized as a response to certain specific events. For instance, the *Sumi Totimi Hoho* was formed in 1983 after a rape incident with the purpose to tackle such crimes against women and safeguard the rights of women. The different women's organizations in the State are also earnestly engaged in efforts to fight social evils in the society like alcoholism, drug abuse, etc., besides acting as vanguards for women's rights. In fact, under the initiative of the Nagaland Baptist Council of Churches (NBCC) and the different women's organizations in the State headed by the NMA, the State Government was pressurized into passing the Nagaland Liquor Total Prohibition Bill in 1994.

Naga women's organizations also engage in efforts to mediate as peace-makers in conflict situations. Traditionally in Naga society, women acted as arbitrators in times of conflict. Women played the role of peace-makers, for instance, in the pitched battles between their village of birth and the village they married into, they would enter the battlefield holding up a long "Y" shaped stick, and stop the war. Since they were related to both parties by blood and through marriage, neither side could harm them.[23] Today, the women's organizations in Nagaland are somehow continuing this tradition in other forms. As a matter of fact, it is in their role as mediators for peace that Naga women's organizations rose to prominence. A brief look at the activities of the Naga Mothers Association (NMA) throws light on how women in Naga society are somehow carving out spaces in the predominantly male preserves of public life through their peace agenda. The NMA came into existence with the aim of upholding womanhood, to serve as a channel of communication for Naga women's mutual interests and welfare, and to fight against social evils prevailing in the State. From its very inception, the NMA has been fighting for the cause of peace. In October 1994, NMA formed a peace team to stem the deteriorating political situation as a result of the conflict between the Armed Forces of India and the 'National workers' of the Naga national movement, who had been engaged for more than six decades in a fight for Naga independence. With the theme 'Shed no more blood', the NMA initiated dialogues with the 'Undergrounds' and the Government of India to arrest violence and bloodshed. The Naga women have also tried to advocate the notion of neutrality in the concept of motherhood in order to facilitate their intervention in the conflict situation. The NMA, apart from protesting against violence, actively work to fight social evils like drug abuse, and alcoholism as an integral part of the struggle of the Naga people to take responsibility for their political, economic and social rights. They are involved in the treatment and rehabilitation of drug addicts and alcoholics. Likewise, other Naga women organizations have over the years evolved from being mere socio-cultural organizations into political entities, capable of negotiating for space in the institutionalized political process through calls for peace and efforts to stop the violence in the society. The activities of the NMA highlight the ways in which Naga women have appropriated a public role in the society which up till then was regarded as a men's domain and denied to them.

While women in Naga society have made great strides in almost every field, their traditional role in the formal arena of governance has, however, remained largely unchanged. The reality of the matter is that despite an apparent veneer of 'modernization' especially in the urban areas, all Nagas still derived their identity from a village which constitutes their focal reference point. Notwithstanding the differences in lifestyles of the people, all share a common heritage of customary law encompassing the critical concerns of inheritance and laws of governance which continued to determine the gender roles greatly. In spite of the manifold changes taking place in Naga society particularly due to the influences of Christianity, western education and the process of globalization at large, the patriarchal ethos and principles of the Nagas are still firmly rooted and strictly adhered to.

Within such a transitional situation, it is important to critically understand the conflict between dynamics of change and continuity which is reflected in the wider Naga society at present.

REFERENCES

1. *Each Naga tribe has its own name for the institution of Bachelors' dormitory. The Ao Nagas call it 'Ariju', the Angami Nagas call it 'Kichuki', and the Konyak Nagas call it 'Ban', and so on. Morung is believed to be an Ahom word which refers to the Naga traditional institution which was responsible for indigenous Naga education. However, latest research traces the origin of the term to the Konyak Nagas.*
2. Shishak, A.; *Nagas and Education*, Nagas 90, Kohima, 1990, p. 27
3. Imchen, Panger; *Ao Naga Religion and Culture*, New Delhi, 1993, p. 150.
4. Kiremwati, *Education and the Nagas*, Kohima, 1995, p. 11.
5. Downs, Frederick S., *The Christian impact on the Status of Women in North-East India*, Shillong, 1996, p. 48.
6. Census of India 2011, Provisional Population Totals Nagaland Series 14, Directorate of Census Operations, Kohima, Nagaland.
7. Majumdar, P.K, R.P. Kataria, *The Constitution of India*, Allahabad, 1996, p. 186
8. Mills, J.P., *The Ao Nagas*, Bombay: Oxford University Press, 1973.
9. Clark, Mead, *Ao Naga Women*, Boston, 1896.
10. Horam, M., *Social and Cultural Life of the Nagas*, New Delhi: Low Price Publications,1977.
11. Hutton, J.H., *The Angami Nagas*, Bombay: Oxford University Press, 1969.
12. Horam, M.; *Naga Polity*, New Delhi, 1975, p. 46.
13. Longchar, Imtilemla, *Portrayal of Women in Drama*, Dimapur, Nagaland, 1999, p. 32.
14. Zehol, Lucy; *Women in Naga Society*, New Delhi, 1998, p. 2.
15. Ao, Talitemjen, *Ao Naga Customary Laws*, Mokokchung, 1980, p. 63-65
16. *Every Ao village is a democratic Republic in which a citizen irrespective of rank and wealth has the right to participate. But only the male members*

perform the role of citizens. The administrative body of the village is known as Putu Menden, and it is constituted by chosen representatives of different clans.

17. Tongue, M., in No. 14, p. 31.
18. Christina, K. in Thomas, C. Joshua, Gurudas Das, (ed.), *Dimensions of Development in Nagaland*, New Delhi: Regency Press, 2002.
19. Downs, F.S., *The Christian Impact on the Status of Women in North-East India*, Shillong, 1996, p. 20.
20. Longkumer, Limatula; *Christianity and Naga Women in Transforming Theology for Empowering Women*, edited by R.L. Hnuni, Jorhat, 1999, p. 61.
21. National Family Health Survey India; International Institute for Population Studies, Mumbai, India, 2002, p. 53.
22. Tajen Ao, *Ao Naga Customary Laws*, Mokokchung, Nagaland, 1980, p. 48.
23. Shimreichon, Luithui., *Women for Peace in Nagalim*, NPMHR Publication, Winter 2000-2001, New Delhi, p. 3-4.

4

Naga Women and Pattern of Political Participation

Historically women in Naga society had always been accorded a secondary place in governance of their society. Although changes are visible in the social life of the Nagas, mainstreaming gender as an institutional and cultural transformative process to eliminate gender biases in governance and to make it more gender inclusive still remains elusive. Public policies were formulated and executed largely by men. Consequently, women's issues are hardly articulated, much less addressed. Such continuing bias against women, embedded in societal structures, leave women in a state of political powerlessness bringing into sharp focus the need for enhanced political participation by women in the State. The political participation of women remains a leading issue in most modern democracies. While voting is generally accepted as the standard expression of political participation, it also includes activities such as taking part in electoral campaigns, discussing politics, active membership in different political organizations or parties, petitioning the government on specific issues, taking part in demonstrations, etc. The most fundamental dimensions however, of political participation in a democracy, are voting, contesting in elections, campaigning and political membership. These four dimensions form the basis for basic participation in public affairs by the citizens. To utilize these given democratic rights in a proper perspective requires political socialization of the citizens. The views of many theorists of democratic politics suggest that the participation of citizen is absolutely vital to the well-being of the polity. Democracy in its true essence demand that all sections of population be informed about and take interest in politics. This would result in increasing participation of citizens in decision-making. People's participation lends legitimacy to the political system. It is also the essence of liberty and freedom. Prior to the democratic revolution of the eighteenth and nineteenth centuries, people were indifferent and apparently apathetic to the government that ruled. The individual was a passive object and not a participating citizen. It was the instrumental theory of classical liberalists of the eighteenth century who analyzed political participation as a 'natural right'. Participation came to be understood as a means for the defence of the individual and group interests. Due to the general acceptance of the principle of popular sovereignty by democratic and dictatorial regimes, people were encouraged to have political involvement. It was understood that if political power is derived from the people, the people should be involved in politics to exercise their sovereignty.[1]

United Nations International Human Rights instruments unequivocally affirm that women are entitled to enjoy all the rights and freedom on the same basis as men. Women's equal participation is essential to the conduct of democratic elections. At the practical level, an election fails to comply with international obligations and standards unless the opportunity for full and equal participation by women is provided. Equality in all spheres is inseparable from active political participation and is integral to the progress of women. Without active and continuous participation of women at all levels of government, including local party structure, equality in true sense will continue to remain deceptive.

According to the Committee on the Status of Women in India (1974), three main indicators can be used to assess political status of women viz.: (i), their participation in the political process as voters and candidates in elections; (ii), their Political attitudes such as awareness, commitment and involvement in politics and autonomy in political action and behaviour; (iii), their impact on the political process. In the context of the Naga women, the main indicators used to assess the political participation of Naga women were, their participation in the political process as voters and candidates in the elections, their involvement in electoral campaigns and membership in political parties.

Political Socialization of Naga Women

Socialization is the process by which people learn attitudes, motivations, and behaviours commonly considered appropriate to their social positions and the process by which they are reminded of that learning throughout life. Through socialization, one may internalize, or accept as correct, these attitudes and behaviour. Political socialization refers to how individuals imbibe political attitude, motivations and behaviours. The purpose of political socialization in a democracy is to develop citizens who are politically knowledgeable and who actively participate in the decision-making process. This participation primarily involves taking part in the electoral process. Political socialization involves the study of certain agents of influence and change on the individual as he or she learns to participate in the governance of society. Political values, attitudes, knowledge and information are transmitted by different agents like the family, education, peer group, and secondary groups such as the media and political parties.

By the very nature of the Naga traditional social structure, there was a lack of conscious effort at political socialization of the women because governance of society had always been the sole preserve of the males. Naga women had been socialized in ways that promote the stereotype of women as followers, supporters or performers, not leaders or equal partners, within their homes and outside them. Consequently, women's lack of participation in decision-making extends beyond the public to the private sphere. Naga women were relegated to the fringes of governance and polity matters. Women remained largely oblivious about most political affairs considering it men's business. As such, Naga women never received the due political socialization which subdued their interest in political participation and the governance of public life. Today, under the present democratic political system and the rapid increase in literacy and education, women in the State were increasingly exposed to the political functioning of the State through many agents such as the mass media which includes newspapers, television, radio and magazines, besides peers and various institutions. Even though the traditional social structure of the Nagas that excluded women from the political arena were still firmly in place, modern democratic principles and ethos are the norms of the day which legally permitted women as well as men to participate equally in politics. The question of just how far has the modern polity, institutions and values swayed the Naga women in developing interest or otherwise in the political processes of the State and nation as a whole hence become a pertinent query. A look at the agents and processes that induce the Naga women and girls to develop an interest in and participate in political activities provided some insight into the current political socialization process in society.

A recent study[2] brings to light that fourteen per cent of the Naga women were motivated by their parents to be politically interested, while fifteen per cent of them developed an interest because of some political events *via* the mass media. The important role that family played in influencing a woman's political orientation was not surprising given the kinship-based societal system that characterizes Naga society. More importantly, the influence of the male elders in the family was pre-eminent in Naga women's political decisions. Peer influence in development of interest in politics was negligible at just one per cent. For six per cent of the women it was a desire to serve society that got them interested in politics. Another twenty one per cent cited personal interest. Five per cent of the women stated that they had no interest at all in politics with a further thirty eight per cent of the respondents opting not to respond to the question. This in all probability can be interpreted as a general lack of interest in any political activities either. So altogether forty three per cent, i.e., almost half of the respondents exhibited a lack of interest in politics.

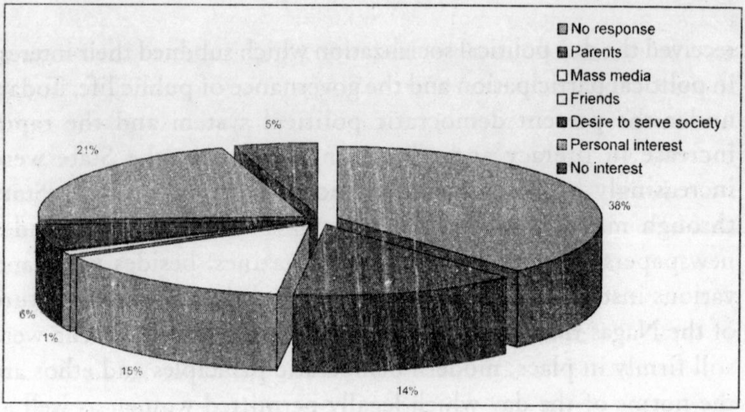

Fig. 4.1: Motivating Factors for Joining Politics

The influence of the mass media as an external agent of political socialization is, therefore, optimal amongst the women. This aspect can be viewed in light of the fact that in the modern era of mass communication and technology, media has become an important and indispensable agent of change. It played a crucial role in shaping voters' interest in and attitudes about an election. It can change not only the mindsets of the individuals in creating interest in politics, but also the entire society, creating a new situation. The way the media portray women, how they deal with issues of special concern to women, and whether they convey effectual voter education messages can have a major impact on women's participation in an election. By gradually shaping public opinion, personal beliefs and even people's self-perceptions, media influences the processes of socialization and shapes ideology and thinking. So, the primary function of media was to build up gradually and inadvertently an awareness of the basic elements in the political system.[3] In Nagaland, the most popular form of media was the newspaper. The radio and television was not a very commonly used form of media among the Naga people as far as political news was concern. Political parties used the print media to engage the electorate in their own interests. The fact that mass media assumed the primary role as the agent of political socialization of women in the State was not surprising given the fact that politics was considered to be men's business and, hence, the primary political socialization process normally bypassed the girls and women. Whatever news and information were gleaned from the mass media formed the base of political knowledge for most women. So the role of the media became very crucial in creating the political consciousness and subsequent participation of Naga women.

Naga Women as Candidates in the State Legislative Assembly Elections

The Indian Constitution provides for a representative and parliamentary form of democracy making elected representatives responsible to the people. It gives the right to adult citizens to elect their representative periodically. The framers of the constitution endeavoured to make Indian democracy, the 'Government of the people'. The electoral process, therefore, assumes an integral position under the democratic political framework. Since Nagaland attained statehood on 1st December 1963, eleven General Assembly Elections to the State Legislature have been held. At present there are sixty constituencies represented in the Nagaland Legislative Assembly. The state of women representation in the Nagaland State Legislature presents a very negative picture. Since the first election to the State Legislative Assembly conducted in 1964, not even a single woman has been elected to the State Legislature.

Table 4.1: Men/Women Candidates in the State Assembly Elections 1964-2003

Year of Election	Total seats contested	No. of Male Candidates	No. of Women Candidates	Percentage of Women Candidates	No. of Women Elected
1964	40	73	Nil	—	Nil
1969	40	144	2	1.38	Nil
1974	60	207	Nil	—	Nil
1977	60	303	Nil	—	Nil
1982	60	245	Nil	—	Nil
1987	60	214	3	1.40	Nil
1989	60	140	Nil	—	Nil
1993	60	178	1	0.56	Nil
2003	60	225	3	1.33	Nil
Total		**1729**	**9**	**0.52**	**Nil**

Source : Reports on the General Assembly Elections of Nagaland, 1964-2003, Government of Nagaland.

Starting from the first general Assembly Election in 1964 to the tenth Assembly Election held in 2003, there had been only nine women candidates (two of whom contested twice), out of a total of 1,729 candidates[4]. This accounted for a mere 0.5 per cent of the total candidature. Further, an analysis of the performance of the women candidates with regard to the votes secured in the elections suggests that the attitude of the Naga electorate towards women in governance was not favourable. This is amply illustrated by Figure 4.2.

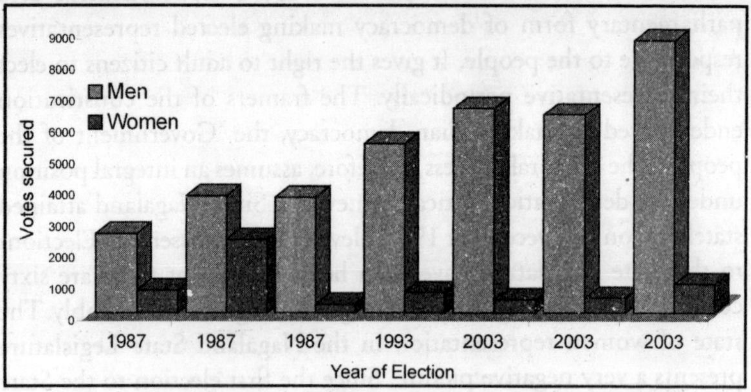

Fig. 4.2: Performance of Women Candidates in the Nagaland Legislative Assembly Elections, 1987-2003

Figure 4.2 clearly indicates the wide margins between the numbers of votes secured by the women candidates as against the winning (male) candidates. For instance, during the sixth General Election in 1987, in the three constituencies of Peren (7A/C), Arkakong (22A/C) and Bhandari (40A/C), the women candidates could secure only 729, 2350 and 271 votes respectively as against the winning male candidates who could secure 2,548, 3,747 and 3,698 number of votes respectively in these three constituencies. This showed that none of the three women candidates could secure more than 27.35 per cent of the total votes. The performance of the women candidates were no better in the other years too. Election records revealed that where women candidates had been fielded by the political parties as candidates, they were usually put up in a constituency where the party position was tenuous, or where the opposing candidate had a very strong foothold and was widely predicted to emerge as the winner. A case in point was the candidature of Ms. Chubalemla being put up by the Nagaland People's Front (NPF) party in the 2003 General Assembly Election against Mr. S.C. Jamir, a stalwart of the Nagaland political scene. As a larger than life presence in Naga electoral politics and a three time Chief Minister and the incumbent of the Chief Ministerial office at that time, his influence and hold on the constituency (22 Aonglenden A/C) was unquestionable, and therefore, his winning the election was a foregone conclusion. Predictably, he won the election by a wide margin. An examination of the party position in connection with the candidature of the other women candidates too exhibits a similar scenario as the above mentioned case. Thus, the role and conviction of the political parties of Nagaland, which were all dominated by male politicians, in fielding women candidates remains questionable.

A crucial factor that worked against the women candidates in the Naga electoral process was the double standards of 'morality' employed to assess the characters of the women candidates. Ironically, while the personal characters of the male politicians were a non-issue at any point of time, it assumed magnified proportions and became the subject of widespread speculation for a female candidate. In fact, when the candidacy of any woman was projected, issues of her 'morals' and 'character' immediately became a matter of scrutiny by the concerned political leaders as well as the electorate at large. Such prevailing culture of double standards employed against the women candidates was a clear manifestation of the patriarchal ethos that seeks to keep women subordinate and out of the power arena by the male-centric Naga society.

Women and Political Parties in Nagaland

Political parties are without doubt among the most important institutions affecting women's political participation. Most candidates depend on parties for their nomination, their base of electoral support and help during the election campaign, financial resources, and continued assistance even after elections. Often Political parties control decisions about who will be nominated to run for office, what positions candidates will be given on the party lists, and who will receive support during campaign and after the election. The role of political parties is, therefore, critical in determining the prospects of women aspiring to public office. Political parties may also determine the extent to which issues of special concern to women become part of the State or national political debate and are given serious considerations in the work of the legislature. In fact, the role of political parties in the political participation of women assumes immense significance because political parties are considered to be the main vehicle to increase women's mobilization and are important tools of political empowerment. Political participation is not mere exercise of franchise by the citizens. Membership in political parties is another significant pointer to their political participation. While exercise of one's franchise can be a one-time act of political participation, membership in political organizations is a more sustained form of participating in the political system. For any intending candidate, whether a woman or man, the most common route to elected office was through political parties. Particularly for a woman, entrée into politics can be a colossal task without the backing of a political party. Hence, women seeking an entrée into politics must necessarily be affiliated to one political party or the other.

Political parties vary greatly in the extent to which they seek to promote women into leadership positions and to recruit women as party candidates, as well as in the extent to which they address political, economic and social issues of special concern to women. The political membership of women in Nagaland remained extremely low. Only fourteen per cent of the Naga women had primary membership in some political parties, with a whooping eighty-six per cent of them not having membership in any party. For those women who had membership in political parties, Ideology was cited as the most widespread deciding factor for joining a political party. Leadership also formed another important factor for joining the party.

In addition to the negligible representation of women within political parties in the State, it emerged as a matter of concern that only eight per cent of the women opined that their views and opinions were valued within their respective parties, while six per cent of the women perceived receiving biased treatment within their party with their standpoints and opinions not accorded due respect in their parties.

An insight into the familial attitude towards women in active membership in political parties can be seen through the fact that most of the women having primary membership in political parties candidly admitted that their families were not keen about their decision to join politics. In the case many woman family members had in fact voiced reservations as well as apprehension regarding their decision. This undoubtedly implied that the notion of women in politics do not receive societal approval in Naga society. Of the very few Naga women who had political membership, only a handful of them were in the upper echelon of the party hierarchy. Most of the women members in the political parties were engaged in running errands, cooking and serving the male members during elections or any important party meeting or gatherings. Therefore, despite their entry into political parties it was to be seen that for the Naga women, far from being elevated to positions of decision making processes, their conventional role of domesticity was actually transferred into the political arena. Ultimately, mere membership in political parties did not guarantee the Naga women a place in decision-making.

At the same time, it is recognized that if Naga women were not active within political parties as the primary channel of political recruitment, however, lowly their perceived contributions to it may be presently, they may fail to acquire the political skills, social networks, and political experiences that were invaluable for gaining access to higher levels of elected and appointed office. Further, in the absence of adequate gender representation within political parties women tended to be marginalized from the political processes including the decisions on the fielding of party candidates during elections. This aspect clearly comes to light when we trace the pattern of candidature and the subsequent performance of women candidates in the general elections of the State.

Table 4.2: Pattern of Candidature and Performance of Women Candidates Party-wise (1987-2003)

Sl. No.	Year	No. and Name of Constituency	Name of Women Candidate	Party	Votes Polled	Total Votes Polled
1.	1987	7 Peren A/C	Sebeule	IND	729	9353
2.	1987	22 Arkakong A/C	Chubalemla	NNDP	2320	8606
3.	1987	40 Bhandari A/C	Lochumlo	IND	271	8808
4.	1993	37 Tyui A/C	R.L. Kinghen	INC	652	10648
5.	2003	3 Dimapur 111 A/C	Anupama Mech	IND	427	14221
6.	2003	5 Ghaspani 11 A/C	Akheli	IND	486	20979
7.	2003	26 Aonglenden A/C	Chubalemla	NPF	928	9674

Source: Reports on the General Assembly Elections of Nagaland, 1987-2003, Government of Nagaland.

The role of political parties in the failure of successive women candidates come into focus based on the fact that out of the seven women candidates, four (i.e., 57.12%) of them were independent candidates, with the remaining three women being affiliated to the Naga National Democratic Party (NNDP), Indian National Congress (INC), and the Nagaland Peoples' Front (NPF) parties. This scenario, where a good majority of the women contested as Independent candidates and not fielded by any political organization in itself highlighted the attitude of reluctance of the political parties themselves towards women as political entities. Without the backing of a political party the chances of any candidate being victorious remains doubtful given the fact that money power played an integral part in the Naga electoral processes.

Election records of the State further show that in the Tenth State Assembly Elections, ten political parties were in the electoral fray, besides some Independent candidates. Out of these, three were regional political parties, while the rest were national political parties. The most important and influential political parties in the State are the NPCC (INC), the NPF, the Bharatiya Janata Party (BJP), and the National Democratic Movement (NDM). The party structure of some of the major political parties of the State at the time of the said election reveals the absence of women from the top party structure. For instance, in the BJP State level working committee, out of twelve members, there was only one woman member[5], holding the post of Secretary[6]. Again, in the list of the Office Bearers of the NPCC, out of twelve members, there was not a single woman member[7]. The case was no different in the other political parties of the State. The absence of women at the top echelons of party structure is symptomatic of the marginalization of women from the power centres of decision-making in the political parties. The low gender visibility in the decision-making hierarchy of the political parties in the State was an indication that the political parties were themselves conservative with regard to notions of gender-equity.

All political parties in the State did have a women's wing, such as the Mahila Congress of the INC, the NPF Women's Wing, etc., but access to the inner ring of the party, which was the core of the power structure was generally denied to women. Therefore, establishment of special wings for women while providing an avenue for Naga women to become active, learn political skills and develop networks within the party if they are linked directly to party leadership, may also inadvertently lead to the compartmentalization or marginalization of women within the party. In the context of the Nagaland electoral scene, the presence of a few elite women in the political parties was not expected to make a big difference in the larger political set-up, unless women at the grassroots were politically empowered. In particular, issues related to the problems of women cannot be taken up seriously in the absence of more women at important posts of decision-making in the party hierarchy which remained male dominated at present. A study on Women in Public life, carried out by the United Nations Division for the Advancement of Women (DAW) argues that only a critical mass of women allows female politicians to bring different values to public life. In the absence of numerical strength of women within the party hierarchy of the political parties in Nagaland, though the parties may champion the cause of women in their manifestoes, during elections, party tickets invariably seemed to be issued only to men. For instance, the Nagaland Peoples' Front (NPF) showed some concern for women's welfare in their election manifesto for the Tenth General Election to the State Legislative Assembly wherein manifesto No. 13 says: *"We shall create a separate Women's department to develop their welfare and provide opportunities for self-employment"*.[8] However, despite their professed concern for the cause of women upliftment, they fielded only one woman candidate, albeit unsuccessfully, in the said election which belied their apparent claims of championing for women. Of course, in their defence, the party, when they came to power did indeed set up a Women Development Department whose effectiveness or otherwise is yet to be felt in the State. The criterion for political parties in the State for their selection of candidates is their 'win ability' factor, rather than their contribution in the constituency, which were purportedly carried out mostly by the women activists. Most political parties den,· Naga women candidates their tickets on account of their 'non-win ability' factor, which effectively ensures male patriarchal domination in the political arena of the State.

With the right political will in the State there is no reason why the number of Naga women in the political party structure cannot be enhanced through certain strategies and mechanisms. Many countries have a law regulating how political parties must be organized and registered and also dictating how they must operate. Specific provisions aimed at enhancing women's political participation can be included in political party laws. For instance, they can affirm their party position on gender equality in the party constitution. They can also mandate that party management and party policies are made gender-balanced. Alternatively, government could also adopt measures to encourage parties to field more women as candidates by offering benefits such as additional campaign financing to parties nominating greater number of women. One of the most effective ways to ensure women are elected to office is to require that party candidate lists be gender balanced or include certain proportion of women. For example, the election law of Bosnia and Herzegovina includes provision requiring that men and women each constitute at least a third of the candidates listed.[9] If appropriately applied, such measures can broaden democracy and ensure enhancement of the political participation of Naga women.

Naga Women as Voters

In a democratic system, participation in politics has to be viewed at the levels of acquisition and exercise of power and exercise of the rights of a citizen. As such, voting is accepted as the standard expression of political participation. The voting pattern is an expression of power which an individual is entitled on account of constitutional framework. It is also an expression of an ideology and understanding which a person has. Voting can act as a catalyst in bringing change in the political and social milieu. An analysis of the participation of the electorate in Nagaland during four Assembly Elections held in 1987, 1989, 1993, and 2003 offers a quantitative measure of political participation by the Naga women.[10] Figure 4.3 indicates that the Naga women were very active in terms of voting in the elections. In fact, according to the statistics, it revealed that in two consecutive years, i.e., 1987 and 1989, women voters outnumbered the male voters in the State with 85.9 per cent and 86 per cent of votes as against 83.2 per cent and 85.3 per cent of male voters respectively. This showed a higher margin of 2.7 per cent and 0.7 per cent voters in favour of women voters. It is a clear indication that there is no significant gender gap between men and women, as far as voting is concerned.[11]

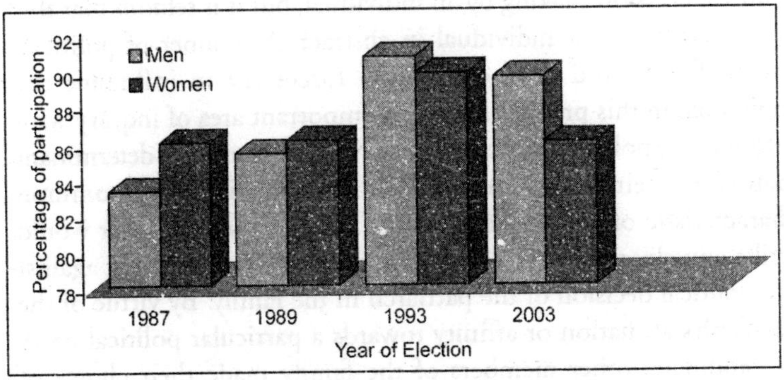

Fig. 4.3: Participation of Men/Women Electorate in the Nagaland Legislative Assembly elections (1987-2003)

As a matter of fact, exercise of one's franchise appears to be one political exercise which women performed enthusiastically in the State. The present study shows that seventy-five per cent of the women respondents had exercised their franchise in the Tenth General Assembly Election. However, this aspect has to be viewed in the light of performance of women candidates in the same elections. For, despite the heavy turnout of women voters, the ominous fact remained that, none of the women candidates were elected to office. This reflected the negative attitude of the electorate in general towards women as partners in matters of governance and decision-making process. Though women constituted a majority of voters on some occasions as per election records, the outcome of the election obviously throws up the fact that most of them did not vote in favour of the women candidates. This leads us to two possibilities. Firstly, if these women voters were acting on their own volition, then it can be an indication that Naga women could not get over the notion of seeing men in the decision-making seats and were culturally conditioned to believe that only males could wield political authority. Secondly, women voters do not exercise independent voting, i.e., they could be voting according to the dictates of their male family members. Hence it becomes important to look into the determinants of voting pattern of the women in the State.

To vote for a particular person or political party is a process of political decision-making by an individual, but it is seldom that this is performed by an individual in abstract. A number of political, social, family and even communal forces try to influence the individual in this process. So, a very important area of inquiry with regard to the political participation of Naga women is the determinant factors of their voting pattern. The most obvious and common characteristic of voting behaviour of the Naga women that would strike any close observer was the fact that they rarely voted against the political decision of the patriarch in the family. By virtue of the patriarch's affiliation or affinity towards a particular political party or candidate, other members of the family made their choice of candidates or party accordingly. There was no scope for the exercise of the individual right to make objective political decisions in the light of such a practice which was conventionally followed and taken for granted. As per the patriarchal social structure and norms that existed in Naga society, a woman normally did not have the autonomy to make independent decisions regarding her choice of candidates to vote for.

Almost in conjunction with the above determinant, the voting decision of Naga women was also determined to a great extent by kinship ties. In Naga society, clans are the primary and primordial kinship units. Often, clan loyalty surpasses other familial and affinal relationships amongst the Nagas. So consideration of kinship played a crucial role in determining the voting pattern of any Naga. When kinship relations came to the fore during elections, considerations of party affiliation became secondary for most Nagas. Clan decisions were invariably made by the male members leaving the women with no option but to follow suit or else face censure from her clansmen.

Voting along traditional party lines was another practice widespread among the Naga electorates. This implied that a particular family would traditionally extent support to, and vote for a particular party, irrespective of the candidates' capabilities, or issues taken up by the party. They vote for that particular party because they had always done so. Here too, the choice of the party almost always depended on the patriarch of the family. This practice too does adversely affect the women candidature like in the above stated instances. In the rural areas, village leadership was a major influencing factor that impinged on the voting decision for both men and women. In many cases, during the election time, there were reported cases of the village leadership taking the decision to support a particular candidate or political party. These decisions were often made public and sometimes even announced through the media. In certain cases, once such a decision was made, the village leadership may even resort to forcefully preventing the other opposition parties from entering and campaign in their village. This was supposedly done to assure the strongest and undivided support for their chosen candidate. Viewed from a liberal perspective, it can be termed as an unconstitutional practice which infringed upon the political rights of the individual. Very often such collective decisions were made on the basis of some bargain or understanding arrived at between the candidate and the village elders, normally promises of economic development for the village. Practices of this kind were always to the disadvantage of the women candidates who, for various reasons, were as yet to establish firm footing in the administrative and political set-up, and consequently in no position to make tall promises to the electorate.

An extremely negative element of electoral practices in Nagaland was the excessive use of money and muscle power to sway votes. Money was abundantly used to win over votes for one's candidacy and party. Some women who were actively involved in grassroot politics pointed out that without a generous amount of money being doled out, no candidate could ever hope to win an election in the State. In fact, canvassing and campaigns by these women activists primarily involved procuring promises of votes in return for a certain amount of monetary incentive. The *modus operandi* for the women activists, mostly middle-aged women, were to make home visits and convince the head of the family, normally the husband or father (once the husband was won over, the wife would follow suit) to vote for their candidate, then give the family some money on the pretext of this or that purpose. This in general worked among the lower socio-economic sections of the population who formed the major bulk of the population. Election was thus reduced to an opportunity to make some quick buck for a large number of the electorate, rather than being regarded as an instrument to usher in democratic changes in society. Many women became direct or indirect beneficiaries of the pecuniary benefits courtesy of the candidates. Women workers in the lower ranks of the party hierarchy were used for this task of distributing money during the pre-election campaign, and even on the polling day itself. In fact the polling booth behaviour of such women has generated some curiosity and attention among political analysts and academics. The women party workers allegedly played a very significant role on the polling day. On the actual polling day, the women activists were at their ingenious best, in the practice of 'proxy voting', which was rife in the electoral process in Nagaland. According to primary information from some women activists, the practice of proxy voting was executed mostly by them (women). They deployed a number of tactics and strategies to carry out these acts, such as, by repeatedly changing their attire, applying certain substances to remove the indelible ink, or under the guise of serving tea to the polling officers, etc. In this process, they also reportedly kept a watchful eye for the opposition party indulging in the same practice, and put a stop to them should the situation demand. Very often, such acts were purportedly carried out in collusion with the polling officers. The women activists involved in such acts were invariably from the lower socio-economic section of the society. What becomes obvious from an analysis of their polling booth behaviour was a lack of ideological grounding or an understanding of democratic principles of governance. Rather, they were driven by considerations of economic gains and other benefits to be derived out of such actions. Given such a practice, Naga women candidates were in an economically disadvantaged position as compared to their male counterparts because they could not mobilize the huge sums of money required to back such a money-oriented political culture.

Mention needs to be made here of another detrimental factor that works against the women candidates in the State, which was the use of 'muscle power' rampant in the electoral process of Nagaland. Every single election to date had been marred by incidents of violent clashes between the contesting political parties or candidates, often resulting in the loss of valuable lives. In fact, the use of 'money power' and 'muscle power' were almost synonymous with the electoral process of the State which relegated Naga women candidates to a distinctly disadvantaged position.

An account into the determinants of voting behaviour of the Naga electorate in general and the women in particular brings to light that the contemporary trend of the electoral processes in Nagaland was characterized by a very shallow understanding of the democratic principles and values. The democratic rights of the citizens were abused and often took a back seat in the dominant countenance of 'money power' and 'muscle power' which characterized the electoral process in Nagaland. The electorate neither questioned party manifesto nor the credibility of the party or the candidates. Manifestoes, which were supposed to be a political party's plank to power on the basis of issues they accord priority to, became a non-issue in the electoral process of Nagaland. This is exemplified in the Tenth General Assembly Election to the State Assembly, where, a major political party like the Congress Party, i.e., the Nagaland Pradesh Congress Committee (NPCC) in the State did not come up with any Election Manifesto in the State, simply because they did not see the need of it. This clearly indicated the lack of political maturity of the electorate besides undermining the ethics of modern democratic principles which allowed the pre-eminence of other negative factors to play in the electoral process of the State such as the use of money, or muscle power. It in turn led to other negative practices such as staging electoral 'coups'. Carrying out electoral 'coups' by dominant political groups or villages was quite a common practice during polling day in Nagaland which often reduced elections in the State to a democratic mockery. It may be noted that till date no women polling agent had ever been appointed by any political party on the poll day.

The voting dynamics of the women electorate showed, therefore, that, by and large, they did not exercise independent voting being constraint by a number of socio-cultural factors. The electoral behaviour of the Naga women voters further indicate that, with a mind-set that was so used to seeing men in the driving seat of policy-making they were yet to get over the mental block of voting for a man only. Consequently, the dominant characteristic of the electoral system in Nagaland continued to be a lack of political articulation which could override the social, personal and kinship relations and economic considerations. Their voting behaviour was not dependent on particular gender-issues either. Most Naga women considered voting as a ritual to be performed at the bidding of their husbands or elders without bothering about political parties, issues, or the capabilities of the candidates. Hence, Naga women's political participation in their role as responsible voters may be questioned. Under such a social and political circumstance, it remained doubtful whether the right of adult franchise could be used meaningfully by the women of the State to bring about much needed changes in the gender equation of the society.

In order to realize the full potential of democracy there was a need for the women themselves to understand their rights and responsibilities, and must be sufficiently knowledgeable and well informed to cast ballots that are legally valid and to participate meaningfully in the voting process. This may be accomplished through 'Voter Education' and 'Civic Education', which was generally used to describe the dissemination of information, materials and programmes designed to inform voters about the specifics on mechanics of the voting process for a particular election. Civic education is aimed at conveying knowledge of a State's political system and context. Civic education might include information on the system of government, the nature and powers of the offices to be filled in an election, the principal economic, social and political issues facing the nation, the value of democracy, the equal rights of women and men. Voter and civic education can be critical in enhancing women's participation in elections, particularly in a society like the Nagas' where women have not traditionally played an active role in the electoral process. Through voter education, women electorate can be made to understand that 'family voting', which is a practice wherein a family member casts ballots on behalf of the entire family, is not an acceptable practice in democratic elections. Family voting is particularly likely to detract from women's ability to cast individual and secret ballots. In its worst form, family voting constitutes a type of fraud in which women are deliberately deprived of their right to vote. If perpetrated on a large scale, family voting can bring into question whether an election outcome reflects the will of the people.

Women and Electoral Campaigns

Electoral campaigns refer to those activities designed to solicit votes for a particular candidate or party. Taking part in campaigns is another important marker of political participation. One need not be a formal member of any political party to engage in political campaigning. Carried out in the right perspective, political campaigns can be a very effective means of democratic expression. Campaigning can take a number of forms such as organizing rallies or meetings, door to door campaign, or distributing pamphlets and posters. In Nagaland, campaigning can be said to take place at a number of levels. On the highest level, the candidate along with the top party functionaries addressed all the high profile, public rallies. Another level of campaigning comprised of the elite sections of society usually led by the family members of the candidate, whose campaigning would ordinarily be confined to the elite segment of society. At this level, votes are normally garnered on the basis of face value, due to one's connection to some 'important' people. At yet another level, the grass-root campaigning takes place. It was at this level that the 'vote for money' generally takes place. And this was where the women activists played out their 'political' role, not in the lofty arena of decision making. They were used by the candidates to discreetly distribute money and promises of 'favours' on behalf of the candidates among the lower socio-economic section of the society.

Most women in the State abstain abstained from electoral campaigns. For instance, even among the respondents, only ten per cent of them were found to be involved in campaign activities. Significantly, out of this ten per cent of respondents engaged in electoral campaigns, eighty-eight per cent of the women were found to be married. The very low percentage of women involved in electoral campaigns in our sample study is a projection of the larger societal picture which saw very little involvement of women in electoral activities, particularly with regard to campaigns.

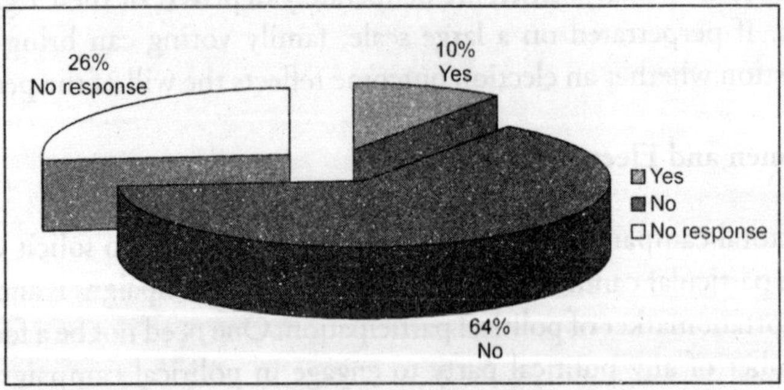

Fig. 4.4: Percentage of Participation in Electoral Campaigns

The reasons for the low engagement in political campaign by the Naga women were many. One of the chief factors was the negative attitude of the society towards politics in general and disapproval of women's political involvement in particular. Besides the deep-seated attitude of society against women in politics borne out of millennia of exclusion of women from the traditional seats of decision-making, the downbeat attitude of the people was also associated to the prevailing view of politics as a 'dirty manipulative game of muscle and money power'. Consequently, women who were active in politics were considered to be of 'easy virtue'. Since politics was viewed as an 'immoral' arena of activity, women's political participation was also accounted for similarly. Such pejorative attitude towards political activities and activists deterred many genuinely interested women from active political participation, especially campaigning. Campaigning required people to be very mobile, physically and spatially, staying out of the house at all the odd hours of the day or even for days at a stretch, as well as interacting with people from all walks of life. Such behaviour did not conform to the Naga people's notion of 'respectable girls', who were expected to be less 'social', and be under the supervision of their parents or elders.

The lack of women legislators in the State is an important, albeit often an overlooked factor for the low rate of female political participation. Studies in the United Kingdom highlights the fact that in constituencies where women are elected to parliament, women were more active as citizens, displaying greater political interest and willingness to help in campaigns.[12]

Another commonplace rationale for the low level of political activity among females in electoral campaigns can be located in the heavy responsibilities of domestic engagements. A Naga woman by and large could not spare time to attend political campaign too, let alone take part in it. Not only was she required to work hard, looking into the needs of everybody at home, but she was also expected to hand down a healthy tradition of hard work to her children by example. Much had been written about the 'freedom' enjoyed by Naga women in the domestic sphere where she appeared to have wide latitude in decision-making and movement. However, the much touted 'freedom' entailed more responsibility than freedom to the extent that the lady of the house would bear all responsibilities should there be any kind of mismanagement of the household. This was amply reflected in the sample study where only nine per cent of the women somehow managed the time to attend political campaigns.

Education and Political Participation

Education is a critical component which helped in raising women's awareness and can be regarded as one of the important instruments of empowering women. Many studies have established the fact that there is a general tendency for women's participation in public affairs to increase with corresponding enhancement of their educational qualification. The literacy rate of the women in Nagaland is one of the highest in the country, standing at 76.69 per cent which is much higher than the all India female literacy rate of 65.46 per cent (2011 census). Considering the high rate of literacy in the State among the Naga women, it was expected that there would be a positive correlation between their level of education and political participation. An analysis of the correlation between educational qualification and political participation of the women, however, presented an entirely different scenario.

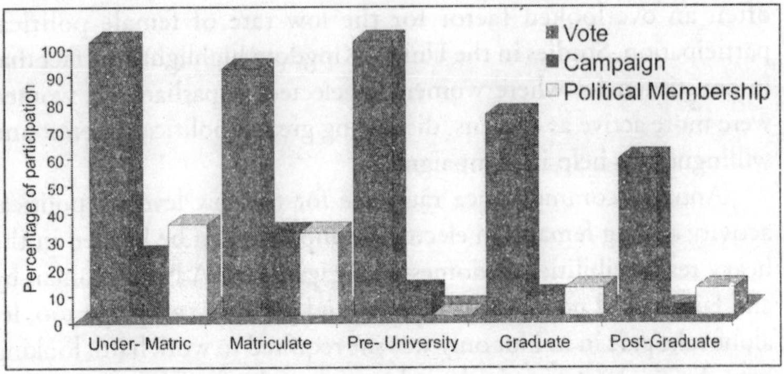

Fig. 4.5 : Political Participation according to Level of Education

An inverse correlation was observed between higher level of education and political participation of Naga women. Whereas women having primary level to matriculate level of education recorded a high participation of ninety per cent to hundred per cent participation rate in voting during the Tenth State General Assembly Election, it soon became apparent that the level of participation gradually declined with the rise in the educational level of the respondents. Seventy-three per cent of graduates had exercised their franchise, followed by a further decline in the participation among the post-graduate respondents with only fifty-seven per cent of them having cast their votes. Similar was the case with regard to electoral campaign. Sixty three per cent of respondents who participated in electoral campaigns were matriculates and below. Only nine per cent of the women with pre-university degrees reported taking part in electoral campaigns, with a further decline seen among the graduates with seven per cent participation. Overall, low to moderately educated women participated more in electoral campaigns. Notable was the absence of any respondent with post-graduate degree from the sample who took part in campaigning.

The same trend was in evidence with regard to membership in political parties. Out of the total of fourteen per cent respondents having primary membership in political parties, sixty-three per cent of them were matriculates and below, ten per cent respectively of women with graduates and post-graduate degrees. These statistics bring to light that the highest political participants were those women having the lowest level of education (under-matriculate) and the least participant were those with higher levels of education such as graduates and above. It clearly showed that the level of political participation declined with the increase in educational levels among the women of the State.

Education is generally expected to create enhanced awareness among the people with regard to their social, political and legal environment. The current political state of affairs of the Naga women showcases a scenario wherein with increasing consciousness about the prevalent corrupt political system, disillusionment sets in among the educated lot. The general trend of electoral processes in Nagaland today characterized by muscle power and excessive use of money and the lack of ideological grounding among most of the electorate is viewed with disdain by the educated sections of society and they rather preferred themselves to keep distance from such activities. Most political parties in Nagaland as it is do not come forward with the agenda of improving the social position of women in their electoral campaigns. So the question of issue-based support from the educated women does not arise for the simple reason that no specific issues are put up. In fact as mentioned earlier the election manifestoes of the various political parties were not accorded any importance by the electorate at large for reasons already enumerated. Besides these factors, many educated women today stressed more importance on becoming economically independent through pursuance of some viable vocation. Economic advancement and independence was regarded by many women as the path to empowerment, rather than active pursuit and participation in politics. Further, in their quest of a career, many educated women do not consider devoting time for political activities worthwhile which demanded plenty of time.

There were still a section of educated people who preferred themselves to keep distance from the 'Indian political system' and the electoral process held under the Indian Constitution. This view was reflected in the response of one highly educated respondent who said: *"I have no interest in Indian politics. When the Nagas are in negotiating table, how I can show interest to their politics, so let solution take place first, then only I'll be able to decide"*.[13]

Marital Status and Political Participation of Women

The marital status of the Naga women proved to be a key variable to the understanding of the nature of their political participation. As discussed in the preceding sections, there was a general assumption that in Naga society, unmarried girls hesitated to venture into the political arena as a consequence of society's negative attitude towards politics. This assumption was indeed validated on an examination of the association between marital status and political participation of the respondents. The figure below highlights the correlation between marital status and political participation of Naga women on the basis of voting, electoral campaigns, and membership in political parties.

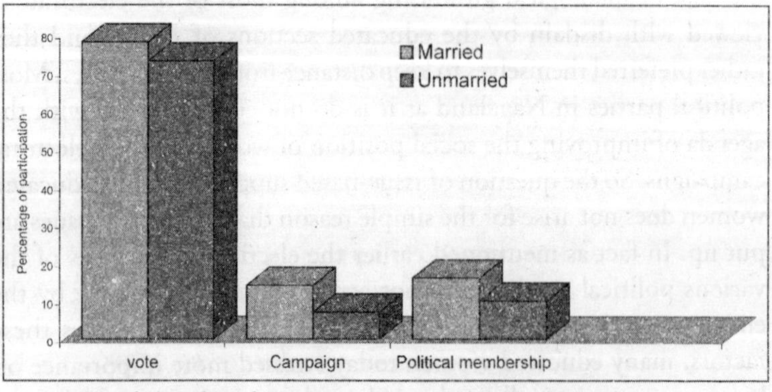

Fig. 4.6: Political Participation according to Marital Status

In all the three components of political participation, i.e., voting, electoral campaign and political membership, the participation of the married women were much higher than that of unmarried women. With regard to voting in the Tenth General Assembly Elections for instance, seventy-eight per cent of the married respondents had participated as against seventy-three per cent of the unmarried women. Membership in political parties of married women stood at sixteen per cent while in the case of the unmarried women it was a mere ten per cent. The picture was no different with regard to participation in electoral campaign. Fourteen per cent of the married women engaged in electoral campaign, while only seven per cent of the unmarried women participated in electoral campaigns.

The significant role of marital status on the political participation of Naga women was further corroborated by the fact that sixty-seven per cent of the women under study subscribed to the same political party or ideology (even if they do not have membership in any political party) as their husbands. This fact suggests that the all important reason as to why more married women were politically more active was largely due to the influence of their husbands. Many Naga women, even those who never exhibited any political interest, did develop an interest after marriage, especially if their husbands were politically active.

Women in Naga society bore a special responsibility for family honour and her behaviour outside the home was a matter of great concern for her entire kin. The ultimate sanction for indiscreet behaviour on the part of young girls was the possibility that no man would wish to marry her and bring disgrace for her family by being left an old maid. This was a common perception in Naga society. Due to such considerations of family honour and respectability, as well as their marital prospects, it was only after marriage that Naga women, even those who were politically inclined could unreservedly participate in political activities without apprehensions of society's censure. It can be inferred here in that marriage provided a secure cushion for Naga women to engage in political activities. Thus, marital status, for a Naga woman, clearly played a pivotal role in determining the nature and extent of her political participation.

Age and Political Participation

Age is one more factor that has an important bearing on political participation of women. Many women are constraint from active political participation due to their child-bearing and rearing roles. Hence, for most women, gender roles associated with reproduction is a decisive factor to their active participation or otherwise in public life. An analysis of the relationship between the age of the women and their political participation in the present work brings out some important pointers on this important aspect.

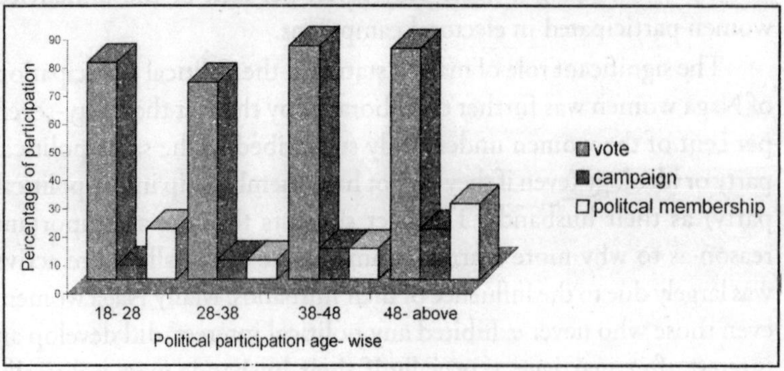

Fig. 4.7: Political Participation according to Age

Figure 4.7 shows the correlation between the different age groups and the political participation of the respondents. For purpose of analysis, the respondents were divided into four age groups, namely, 18-28, 28-38, 38-48, and 48 and above. Except in voting which saw the highest participants from the women in the age group of 38 to 48 years, in all the other dimensions of political action, i.e., political membership and electoral campaigns, the highest participants were from the age group of 48 years and above. Hence, bio-social factors do indeed play a significant role in the level of political participation of Naga women. Women in the age category of 28 to 38 years were ordinarily engaged full-time in establishing a career besides raising a young family which in all probability left them with little scope or time for other demanding activities such as politics. This severely limited their participation in the political arena. The fact that the older age-group showed the highest percentage of political membership further substantiated the assumption that women who were past the child-bearing age were the most politically active.

Women in the age group of 18-28 years were the least active in electoral campaigns at just five per cent. The low rate of participation amongst the youngest age group of girls may be attributed to the fact that Naga girls marry relatively late and, hence, most girls within this age category by implication would be still unmarried. The reasons for the non-participation of young girls are social, as already discussed in the preceding sub-section under the correlation between marital status and political participation. A striking yet ironical fact that emerges is the fact that though most of the women do not actively engage in political activities, yet most Naga women were of the opinion that women should stand for elections and be more politically active. However, this view stands in stark contrast to prevailing situation where only a mere seven per cent of the respondents showed any inclination for the same.

Rural-Urban Differences in Political Participation

Urban areas or towns are characterized by heterogeneity and are generally more cosmopolitan and diverse in nature compared to the rural areas. The means of transport and communications are more developed, people get more media exposure, and hence, exposed to new ideas and concepts. Normally most of the educational institutions like schools and colleges would be concentrated in urban areas. Due to this circumstantial distinctiveness, the urban populace were expected to be more aware about the social and legal issues that concerns them. Likewise, higher levels of exposure to liberal, modern and democratic ideas as a consequence of formal education, media exposure and the general process of globalization as such, the higher political participation of the women from urban areas was presumed to be a foregone conclusion.

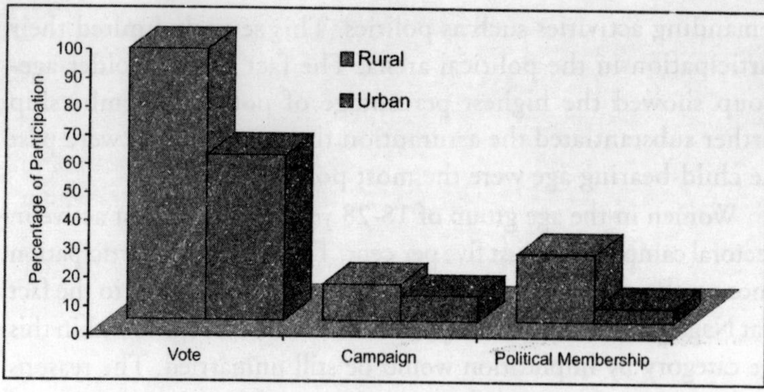

Figure 4.8: Rural-Urban Differences in Political Participation

Therefore, to find that rural women's political participation in terms of voting, political campaigns and political membership exceeded their urban counterparts was in complete contrast to generally held belief. Whereas only fifty-eight per cent of the urban women had exercised their franchise in the Tenth Assembly Elections, the rural women showed a high rate of participation at ninety-five per cent. Again, while only five per cent of the urban women had membership in political parties, twenty-four per cent of the rural women belonged to political parties. There was a noticeable gap between the participation of rural and the urban women with regard to electoral campaign too. Thirteen per cent of the rural women participated in electoral campaigning, which though a small percentage, was still much higher than the participation of urban women which stood at only nine per cent. Many urban women showed either lack of interest or apathy towards this aspect of political activity.

A very important reason for the above phenomenon can be attributed to the fact that in Naga society, village elders were immensely influential in directing the villagers towards the desired course of action. Due to the fact that villages were comparatively sparsely populated with very close inter-personal relationship, the higher level of political participation can be seen as an outcome of the compelling force of the authority of the village elders' collective decisions rather than due to a real awareness regarding political processes on the part of the rural women. Because of the communal nature of the Naga villages very often community decisions under the authority of the village council superseded individual will. Such practices leave little scope for individual exercise of modern democratic rights and hence women, particularly in the rural areas had no autonomy over their political actions and behaviour. The apparently higher level of political participation of rural women in Naga society cannot be assumed to be the actual reflection of democratization of the political processes of the State.

Life in the towns and cities, on the other hand, was beyond doubt characterized by more individualism and thus the primordial relationships were considerably less binding than that of the villages. Though factors of kinship and family relations do certainly come into play even in the urban areas during the electoral process, political participation on a communal level was not the rule as was often practiced in the villages. With more urban women increasingly focused on pursuing higher education and professional careers, they had very little time and inclination to participate in political activities. Since political activities such as electoral campaigning required plenty of time, their pre-engagements in other professional pursuits imposed the problem of time constraints especially among the educated urban women. Moreover, the choice of whether to participate in politics or not was theirs to take, and very often they opted for the latter. Another pertinent factor is the given fact that there exists definitely an inverse correlation between higher level of education and political participation of the Naga women. Since in the field of education women in the rural areas lagged behind their urban counterparts relatively, this was also a significant aspect in the larger spectrum of Naga women's political participation which accounted for the apparently higher participation of the women in the villages.

REFERENCES

1. Tripathy, Swarnamayee, *Political Participation of Women Workers in Orissa*, New Delhi, 2000, p. 4.
2. Jamir, Toshimenla, '*Political Consciousness and Participation of Naga Women: A Sociological Enquiry*' (Ph.D. Thesis), 2007, Nagaland University.

3. Greenstein, F.I, 'Political Socialization' In *International Encyclopaedia of Social Sciences* (ed.), David L., Vol. 13, New York, 1972, p. 554.
4. Since this study was conducted, the Eleventh General Assembly Elections were held in 2008 where four women candidates contested the election; predictably, none of them were elected. Therefore, the omission of the latest Assembly Election in the present work does not in any way change the findings or conclusions of the book.
5. Evangeline Kinimi, Secretary, State BJP.
6. Office of the Bharatiya Janata Party, Nagaland, Kohima, 20th July 2004.
7. Office of the Nagaland Pradesh Congress Committee, Kohima, 4th August, 2004.
8. Election Manifesto of Nagaland Peoples' Front, 2003, Kohima.
9. Office for Democratic Institutions and Human Rights, "Bosnia and Herzegovina: assessment of the Election Law for the 5 October, 2002 elections", (Warsaw, 25 July 2002).
10. We have excluded the General Election held in 1998 because of the total boycott of that particular election by all the opposition parties.
11. Mention may be made here of the culture of 'proxy' voting that is rife in Nagaland electoral processes today. The actual voting percentage might differ slightly from what is projected in the official records.
12. Women's political participation in the UK (http://www.electoral commission.Org.uk).
13. Quotation of the President of Naga Mother's Association (NMA) interviewed on 30th July, 2006. Her statement has to be viewed in the backdrop of the current political crises of the State wherein the people are engaged in a struggle for political liberation from the Indian State. The fight against foreign domination in the Naga Hills started as early as the early part of the nineteenth century. The British foray into the Naga areas contributed to the unity of the Nagas, confronted as they were by an alien rule. The arbitrary division of the Naga territory by the British colonialists for their administrative convenience led to a consciousness that evolved into full-fledged struggle by the early part of the twentieth century. For example, by the Treaty of Yandabo (1826), part of the Naga territory went to Burma (New Myanmar). This sort of division of Naga territory and the systematic encroachment into the Naga territory alarmed the Naga leaders, who

foresaw racial, economic, political and social exploitation. The Nagas expressed their desire for independence to the British administration. In 1929, the members of the Naga Club submitted a memorandum to the Simon Commission stating that they should be left alone to decide and shape their own future. However, the Nagas' desire for self-determination was denied. Furthermore, when India got her Independence, the British Government undemocratically gifted away Nagaland to India and Burma (now Myanmar). Nagaland today, straddling across two countries, is divided by one imaginary international boundary into India and Burma, and is further fragmented into different States and provinces within the said two countries. Thus, in India, the Nagas are fragmented into Manipur, Assam, Arunachal Pradesh and Nagaland. Ever since then, the Nagas have been struggling for their right to self-determination. The formation of the State of Nagaland on 1st December, 1963 did not appease the Naga people. Elections in Nagaland under the Constitution of India were held since 1964. But the Naga people did not participate in the electoral process wholeheartedly, as many view it as an imposition of the Indian rule. Ever since the Government of India and the National Socialist Council of Nagaland-IM (NSCN-IM) signed a cease fire agreement and entered into negotiations in 1997, Naga Civil Societies have also actively participated in the discussions of the Naga political issue, as well as engage in a dialogue with groups from the national movement. Naga women, represented by the Naga Mothers' Association (NMA) had joined in the efforts to consolidate peace in Nagaland.

5
Challenges to Political Participation and Leadership of Naga Women

Women in Naga society are increasingly exposed to modern ideas and concepts due to factors like modern education, media and IT exposure, the globalization process, westernization associated with Christianity, besides others. This in particular was true in regard to ideas of gender equality and women empowerment. But their social reality continued to be constrained by traditional modes of thinking based on a rigid patriarchal value system that had been handed down through the generations. Women were supposed to be the custodians of traditional values and norms, and for this reason, expected to conform to it as well as disseminate it to the younger generations. The pattern of socialization of girls and the social norms of motherhood resulting in the dichotomy of public and private sphere was accountable to a large extent for undermining Naga women's public role. Society socialized its members through different agencies like the family, peer group, educational institutions, mass media and political institutions so that they develop personalities conforming to the social, economic, political and cultural needs of the given society.[1] As a consequence of the notion of women being associated with the domestic sphere, women were generally assumed to evince a low interest in political matters, rarely identify with any political party, and have a low sense of political efficacy. The cumulative effect of all these factors is that women do not have crystallized and independent views on politics and public affairs. It is often believed that women lacked the aptitude to form any views or opinion on political matters and were incapable of evaluating their government or the system.[2] The ability to have informed judgments regarding political functioning and systems may be understood as political awareness in a broad sense. To be precise, political consciousness can be said to be an awareness of political developments, public affairs, and also awareness of gender-deprivation in the political arena. A consciousness or awareness regarding the dynamics of decision-making process is believed to create interest in it. Emphasis presently is focused in particular on the gender-awareness of the women in Naga society as a component of political consciousness because Naga women were a dispossessed lot as far as politics was concerned, being systematically excluded from the traditional governance of society. This had effectively kept many women often ignorant about the political processes of their own society. Awareness regarding their discriminated position in the traditional, social and political structure was expected to engender interest in the modern political arena and stimulate increased participation with a view to bring about positive changes.

Political Efficacy and Aspirations of Naga Women

Women's social setting plays a major role in generating political interest, knowledge and sense of efficacy, and the latter go hand in hand with political participation.[3] Political efficacy is the subjective political competence of women that leads to effective participation. It implies an understanding of the political system which generates self-confidence in the actor. Optimism or pessimism about one's chances to influence the process of decision-making increases or decreases the political efficacy of a woman.[4] Education, urban residence, media exposure and political party affiliation are believed to strengthen the sense of efficacy of women. Confidence in one's political competence is considered essential to stimulate women into participating in the political affairs of the society. Lack of political efficacy, on the other hand, is believed to lead to a stance of indifference or disillusionment which alienated them from the political processes itself. Political efficacy is, therefore, a vital component which enhances political participation. Taking into account the significance of political efficacy, it came as a matter of grave disquiet to find out that women in Naga society were characterised with a very low sense of political efficacy. Only ten per cent of the women in the study expressed confidence that their active participation would contribute to the overall political process of the State, with nineteen per cent of the women actually holding the view that their involvement made no difference at all. A substantial percentage of the respondents, i.e., forty per cent, deigned not to give any response to the query on the same which can be seen as an indication of their unenthusiastic or pessimistic stance regarding their efficacy in affecting the political process of the State.

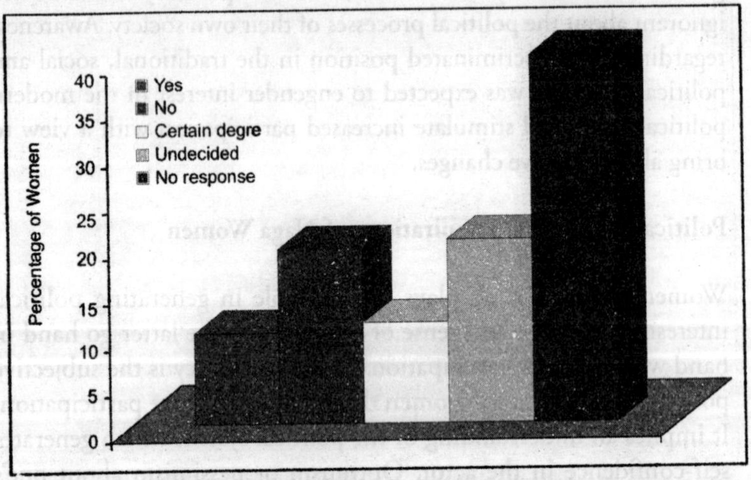

Fig. 5.1: Political Efficacy of Naga Women

The low political efficacy of the Naga women demands consideration in light of their extremely low level of participation in the political process of the State. This state of affairs can be correlated to their ascribed passive role in the traditional political set-up leading to low self-confidence, in all probability a sense of powerlessness, amongst the women regarding their ability to influence the political process. Conscious political socialization and civic education, therefore, becomes crucial to combat the problem of low political efficacy on the part of the Naga women. The pessimistic female political efficacy in Naga society can also be a response to the increasing criminalization of politics in the State. As James D. Wright argues, there are two factors that lead to political alienation and inefficacy: feelings of powerlessness and feelings of distrust.[5] With the overriding elements of 'muscle power' and 'money power' ruling the roost in the Naga electoral practices, women generally felt hapless confronted by such a typically 'masculine' representation of the political activities. It also resulted in a general distrust of politicians and the political system.

Along with low political efficacy another significant pointer to the mode of political participation of Naga women was the decided lack of political aspiration to stand for public office among them. Having political aspiration can be considered as an expression of one's interest and concern with matters of public affairs as well as a move toward political empowerment. It required genuine political consciousness and a desire to engage in decision-making institutions that govern society. Only seven per cent of the women professed they had any political aspirations with a desire to run for political office. An overwhelming sixty per cent had no political ambition at all, while nineteen per cent were undecided about the matter.

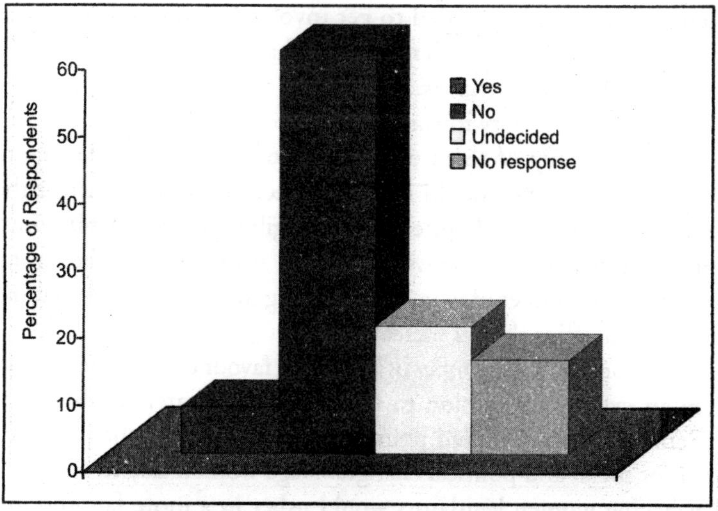

Fig. 5.2: Political Aspiration of Naga Women

The low political aspiration of the Naga women was totally incongruous with the given fact of the demand for political empowerment of women throughout the entire world under the sway of the women's movement. Women all over the globe were clamouring for the right to be part of the decision-making institutions particularly after the UN International Decade of Women. The emergent picture that Naga women showed not the least bit of interest in entering the highest decision-making body in the State do indeed raise questions regarding the social and political environment of Naga society. One key factor for this phenomenon can be accredited to the fact that Naga women had got so attuned to being in the periphery of political activity that it was not easy for them to actually envisage the idea of being in the seats of decision-making themselves. Such perceptions were in turn a definite outcome of stereotype gender roles that was rigidly played out in Naga society under a clear cut sexual division of labour. Hence, there was a pressing call for an alteration in the mind-set and attitude of the Naga society, among the males as well as the females, who needed to break out of the stereotype roles created through the existing social structure. Gender-sensitive education and information was crucial towards this end. Naga women in particular needed to get involved in the public affairs of the State with the understanding that it too was their civic duty as responsible citizens.

Paradoxically, notwithstanding the low political aspirations of the women, many of them were visibly of the opinion that more women in Nagaland should stand for elections and be part of the State legislature. For despite their negligible political aspirations, eighty one per cent of the women in the study were of the strong view that the number of women contesting in elections and running for political office should increase.

The considerable number of women in favour of female legislators were an explicit suggestion to their growing awareness about the present administrative and political system as well as the perceived need for social and political changes. Naga women also strongly felt that having women legislators would usher in a more fair and just society, undoubtedly a positive inference to the increased gender

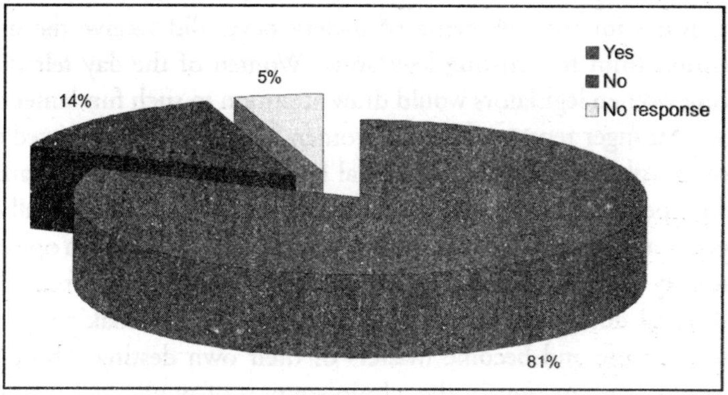

Fig. 5.3: Percentage of Naga Women in favour of Female Candidature

awareness on the part of the Naga women. The rationale proffered for the need of women law makers was wide-ranging and more importantly, significant to an understanding of their gendered perceptions about the prevailing political environment of the State. One suggestion that women were less prone to corruption would not sit too well with the existing male legislators but which would be proved out only with time. This opinion would in fact reflect negatively on the male politicians of Nagaland many of whom were tarnished with allegations of corruption, nepotism and inept functioning. In general, the political system in Nagaland was acknowledged for its corrupt practices which filtered down from the highest level right down to the lowest hierarchy of decision-making and bureaucratic set-up.

There is a strong emergent perception among the Naga women for the need to improve their social and political position in society. It was generally agreed among the women that they were without doubt discriminated on account of their gender, and felt that women legislators would be more understanding and sensitive to gender specific issues. Women's perspective in the framing and implementation of policies was absolutely imperative for the all round amelioration of women's place in Naga society that continued to be characterized by a feudal patriarchal social structure which so often had proven itself to be detrimental to mainstreaming women in public life. Issues like gender-equality, reproductive health, proper water facilities, sanitation, and violence against women including domestic violence, etc., though vital issues for the well-being of society never did receive the due attention from the existing legislators. Women of the day felt that having women legislators would draw attention to such fundamental issues. Stronger representation of women in politics was expected to make possible a review of traditional law in matters like inheritance and property rights, marriage and divorce, custody of children, all of which were heavily biased against women. Many Naga women opined that only then would they be in a position to break free from the traditional dominance of male opinion and decision-making in all spheres of life and become masters of their own destiny. Through increased participation in the administration of public life, women could fight for their rights and privileges, which would ultimately result in "the opposite sex looking upon us as a subjects and not an object".[6] Here, the usage of the term 'objectify' connotes, to depersonalize, to make sub-standard, and to make women not quite human. To objectify is to define a woman in terms of her anatomical and physical attributes.[7] The feeling of being regarded as an 'object' by the males was widespread among the women and was one reason for their low self-esteem leading to lack of confidence required to tackle public situations.

Naga women were known for their aptitude of hard work and enterprising spirit, even to the point of surpassing their male counterparts on this count. A widespread belief popularly held by the women in the State was that they ought to be given a fair chance so that their capabilities could be realized to the fullest possible extent which hitherto was repressed through generations of patriarchy and related norms. This perception should be understood in the sense that given an opportunity, female sensibility would complement the male way of administration as equal partners in all aspects including the governance of their own society. Furthermore, a lot of women favoured the increase participation of women in politics on the grounds that it would open new vistas for women and also encourage more women to come forward and be part of the decision-making process. This reckoning factor had indeed been held conclusive in a study on women's political participation in the United Kingdom (UK).[8] The study revealed that more women representatives may encourage increase participation among women. Hence, strategies to increase the number of women being selected and standing for election may be necessary to address this issue.

In an age where shifting loyalties and horse trading among politicians was more of a rule than an exception, a noteworthy and commendable feature of the few existing women political functionaries in the State was their deep-seated loyalty to the party they were affiliated to. This is quite in contrary to many male politicians of the State who shuttled from one party to another depending upon which political party was more powerful politically and financially, essentially making them 'power-mongers' devoid of any ideological grounding and loyalty. Such practice was not typical of the few women politicians who basically remained loyal to a particular party throughout their political careers. As a matter of fact, in this regard, even in the academic world too there has been a lot of debate about women's politics as different from men. For instance, in a study by Jane freedman, who had been studying French women politicians for ten years, she found that women had a different approach to politics.[9] They were interested in people's everyday life, whereas men were more interested in 'power and going around in big cars'. According to her, women were interested in children, working women, child care, problems of poverty, etc. They were willing to debate the issue and not argue. They were not interested in thumping desks and shouting. They were interested in reaching a consensus. Similarly, from a study of women legislators in Commonwealth countries, C.K. Gariyali describes women's politics as 'the politics of care'.[10] Based on her study, she opined that women's joining in politics was not to acquire power but to bring change in the existing systems, where women were neglected. Her study in the Commonwealth countries also found that women politicians were not interested in confrontational and adversarial politics and politics of winning and losing. Women politicians are found to be interested in the politics of consensus on divergent issues and in finding solutions. Women, by nature are not as aggressive as men. Women are more practical in finding solutions to problems at hand, through the means of co-operation, not confrontations. In Nagaland, the political process in general, and the electoral practices in particular, have over the years acquired a very negative image. It is significant to note that one vital factor that deterred Naga women from politics was the negativity associated with politics. Having more capable women legislators in the legislation is expected to bring about a positive transformation in the image of political activities.

The strong opinions from the Naga women regarding enhanced political participation of women reflected a desire to be respected as individuals in their own right and a growing awareness about their rights as human rights. It may be noted that traditionally, Naga women were identified in conjunction with a male relative—either as a daughter, a wife or a sister. What was visible at present is a growing perception among Naga women to be recognized in their own right as persons who were no less capable than any men in their society. The heightened awareness about their right and the deep sense of deprivation was common to both the rural and the urban women whose opinions do not differ in this regard.

In spite of the progressive and forward looking attitude of many Naga women there are, however, still some elements of conservativeness in the society who held the notion that politics was a men's business and, therefore, it should be left to them. While there were some women who opined that since politics was 'a dirty game' women should stay away from it, yet still there were a few who gave a biblical perspective on why women should not engage in politics. According to them, Christianity held that women were supposed to be simply assisting men and their strength lies in quiet support. Such opinions were infused with religious propensity and a concern that involvement in political activities would leave no time for spiritual life which in all probability would prove to be perilous for the soul. Politics was supposedly a men's game, and a woman's duty was to take care of her family and take care of her domestic responsibilities. This perception typifies the profound impact of Christianity in shaping the life processes of many women in Naga society. Hence, the role of the church is seen to be particularly significant in the way it influenced the nature of political participation or non-participation as the case may be, of the women in the political processes of the State. The church was apparently considered the most important and primary social organization for them by most Naga women. By the same token its role in determining the political participation of the women can be considered crucial in so far as the teachings and structure of the church indoctrinates the Naga Christian's way of life. The structural set-up of the church resembled the patriarchal social set-up of the Naga society where women were relegated to playing only assisting roles thereby placing them in a secondary position within the institutional hierarchy. Though women were enlightened considerably about their rights and worth as human beings through the church, the very fact that its structural set-up was nothing more than a replica of the patriarchal social structure made it difficult for Naga women to reach the top leadership roles in the church hierarchy. Further, the Christian faith advocated its believers to obey without questioning, an element of their faith that made the Naga women accept unquestioningly the lesser place they were assigned in society including in the crucial arena of governance and decision-making.

Women and Political Opportunity

Today there is a definite consensus, internationally as well as through national forums, that political participation is a pre-requisite to enhance the life chances and political status of women. For instance, the Fourth World Conference on Women (1995) recognized that: '*Equality in political decision-making performs a leverage function without which it is highly unlikely that a real integration of the equality dimension in Government policy-making is feasible*'.[11] Further women's groups world-wide insist that unless women become politically visible in the national legislatures, issues that concern them like education, family welfare, domestic violence and healthcare would continue to receive marginal attention.[12] Many consider women's under representation as a reflection of existing unequal sexual division of labour for it seeks to perpetuate the functionalist view of gender whereby women are perceived to be primarily mothers and home-makers. As such political opportunity remains elusive for many women around the globe. By political opportunity, we understand it to be the opportunity available or allowed for women to contest, be part of political decision-making, or to be part of the core committees of political organizations without discrimination on account of their gender. In spite of the constitutional provisions for equal political opportunity, the political structure in Nagaland remains male dominated which subsequently resulted in systematic denial of political opportunity to the women of the State. As was evident from discussions with women political leaders and grass-root activists the present political leaders in the State appeared to have no inclination to make way for their female counterparts. According to some female political activists who had been in the political field for almost three decades, despite talks of gender-equality when the issue of distributing party ticket crops up during the electoral process, the politicians inevitably come up with all sort of excuses to deny giving ticket to women candidates.[13] A common ploy used by the State political leaders was the issue of the 'morality' dimension of candidates which apparently assumed importance only when it concerned women. This yardstick was never applied in the case of men. The bottom line being that the political leaders did not want to displease their male candidates and supporters, and further, they did not accord enough importance to the female candidates, whose 'win ability' factor was always in doubt given the conservative nature of Naga society. They were not willing to sacrifice a constituency for any women candidate whose electoral result was unpredictable in any case. All these factors lead to the systematic denial of political opportunities by the existing politicians of the State even to capable women politicians. This effectively lowered the political status of Naga women in general. As projected in the preceding chapter, the number of women candidates fielded in the elections as well as women in the top level of party hierarchy was grimly low. Such instances reflect the continued denial of political opportunities to Naga women on account of, not their incapability, but their gender.

In view of the above, an effort is made to find out the Naga women's own perception on whether political parties should accord more opportunities to women. The figure below indicates that eighty-nine per cent of women approved the idea, where thirty-seven per cent of them actually strongly felt that women should be given more opportunity. A mere four per cent opined that politics should be left to men.

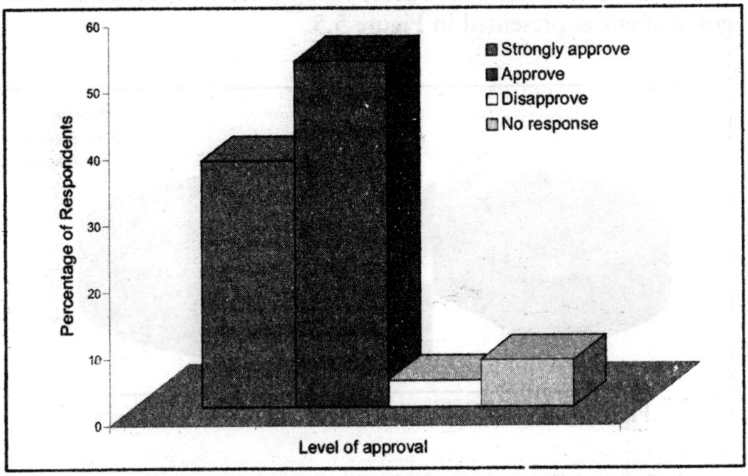

Fig. 5.4: Approval for Enhanced Political Opportunity to Women

The high number of Naga women who wanted to see increased political opportunities to women is reflective of the growing awareness regarding the extent of political deprivation being faced by women in their society. It further indicated that women in Naga society were no less aware about the importance of being part of decision-making in the society. It pointed to a growing political consciousness and the feeling of vulnerability against a social structure that is weighed heavily against them in their quest for meaningful participation in the political process.

Often times it is argued that women are incapable of forming their own independent decisions regarding public and developmental issues. In general it may be a consequence of their lack of awareness or due to lack of interest in social governance. For instance, in order to assess for anyone to the performance of the government they need to be aware about the basic developmental issues and the various schemes taken up and implemented by the State. It also necessitated a basic awareness of the social problems that exist in society. In this regard, our study shows that Naga women are not lacking in knowledge as far as developmental activities of the State government is concerned. Nor are they so ignorant as to be oblivious to the shortcomings of the developmental activities as well. This is amply demonstrated from their response to their assessment of the State government as presented in Figure 5.5.

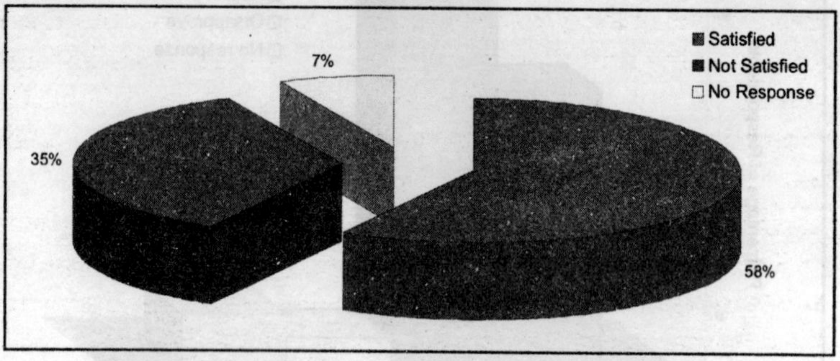

Fig. 5.5: Naga Women's Assessment of State Government

A Statewide survey of Naga women found that fifty-eight per cent of them were evidently satisfied with the present government on the basis of their performance, yet, at thirty-five per cent, quite a substantial number of Naga women were not satisfied with the performance of the State government. Some of the most important constructive achievements pointed out in favour of the government relate to their support of the ongoing peace process between the Naga National Movement Workers and the Government of India. Others pointed to the accessibility factor of the present government to the civil society and the various Non-Governmental Organizations and people's organisations that abound in the State. Some women were happy about the way the government was according importance to the educated unemployed youth of the State by creating opportunities for new talents. The creation of a Department for Women Development by the government was a major factor for approval by the women. Besides these, they were also happy with the development works on roads and drainage systems especially in the urban areas as well as the emphasis on IT education.

Significant failures or lack of achievement of the government according to the women were the misuse of public fund and prioritizing personal interests above public interests. There was also disapproval and recrimination of the government from the Naga women on account of poor management skills as well as pitiable implementation of certain policies, where it was felt, many rightful beneficiaries of the government schemes were not benefiting due to the faulty implementing system in place. Some skeptics of course termed the government as 'more theory, less action', and felt that all their talk of women development were mere lip-service to woo the women voters.

In relation to the nature of priority accorded to different issues by the State government, a slight variation between the rural and the urban women can be observed. While urban women laid more stress on development of basic amenities and infrastructures like roads, communication network, medical and housing aspects, rural women were found to be more concerned with the employment opportunities or lack of it, and related issues. This revealed a shift in the occupation priority of the rural population of the State. Whereas traditionally the people in the villages were principally engaged in farming, today there was a general trend of migration to urban areas seeking better educational facilities for children besides searching for alternative livelihood and employment opportunities, a departure from the traditional means of occupation. The importance accorded by the women from the rural areas to the employment prospects or lack of it as a factor to assess the government can be regarded as another indicator of this growing trend.

Whatever the significant reasons for their failures or achievement might be, it was obvious that the Naga women were certainly not ignorant in the ongoing political and social issues contrary to widespread belief, and they were in fact very vocal and opinionated regarding their views. They were quite aware politically and socially, confident and competent to make their own assessments and judgments on most issues.

Naga Women in Leadership Roles

The essence of patriarchy is male dominance. Naga society exemplifies patriarchy in its highest form when one comes across the traditional political system of governance that continues to operate effectively to date. Not only in governance of public life, but even within the institutional hierarchy of the church which remains one of the most important and influential institutions in the Naga society today, the top leadership positions are always reserved for men. Even capable, experienced and qualified women were able to ascend up in the church hierarchy only up to the post of Associate Pastor, which is basically an assisting position to the Pastor. Within the structural hierarchy of the church all important decisions are made in the Deacon Board which appears like a mirror reflection of the village councils in that it consists primarily of male members. In this apex decision-making body of the church no women can be inducted except a woman Associate Pastor, who, by virtue of her post automatically becomes a member of the Deacon Board.[14]

Though Naga women are rapidly catching up with their male counterparts in almost every field, be it academically, professionally or otherwise, a closer analysis reveal the fact that when it comes to leadership roles, the visibility of women became rather sparse. Structural barriers in Naga society largely account for this phenomenon whereby women are constraint from taking on leadership roles. The complexity faced by the Naga women ranges from constraints on account of their biological and reproductive roles to their social and cultural roles that marginalized them from the public life and effectively relegated them to the domestic sphere. Apart from these structural barriers, another central question is whether the absence of Naga women from leadership roles was also due to their incapability or due to society's non-acceptance of their leadership role. The Naga women's perception on this issue reflected the complexity of the present Naga society with quite a considerable number of the women remaining ambivalent on the issue.

Only thirty-seven per cent of the women were optimistic that Naga people were indeed prepared for women leaders. On the other hand, an almost equal number, i.e., thirty-five per cent of them were not certain whether Naga society was as yet ready to accept women in leadership roles. About a quarter of the women were definite that Naga society was not ready to accept women in leadership roles. The

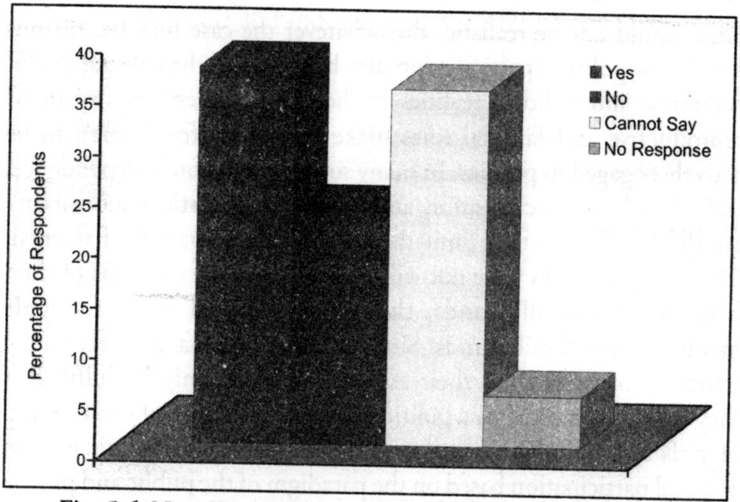

Fig. 5.6: Naga Women's View of Women in Leadership Roles

perplexity and qualms exhibited on the issue is a pointer to the fact that regardless of the progressive laws legislated by the Central Government with the intention of removing the hurdles to women's development and bring them at par with their male counterparts, Naga society remained steeped in age old patriarchal norms and subsequently the mind-set to go with it. While the progressive-minded Naga women fuelled by modern ideas of women's emancipation and empowerment may raise questions regarding their continued denial of opportunities on the basis of the customary laws, nevertheless, they still remained subject to the dictates of traditional customs which stifled their voices for gender-equity. Hence, questions on leadership roles for women brings to the fore the confused and complex state of affairs regarding the position of women in Naga society, torn between forces of tradition and modernity.

Barriers to Political Participation of Naga Women

The problem of political participation of women can differ from one society to the other. What is true for women in other parts of the country and elsewhere may not necessarily be the case in Naga society and its women. Therefore, to make a broad generalization of the same would not be realistic. But whatever the case may be, reasons for the low political participation may be sought in the cultural, socio-economic and political realities of the women. Generally, women's reproductive and familial roles make it difficult for women to be actively engaged in politics. In many societies, economic dependence, lack of political socialization and women's domestic responsibility are the key factors that limit the political participation of women. Also, many families were not willing to finance the elections of their women from family funds, though they would do so for male members from family funds. Since most women have no economic resources of their own, their aspirations could only be fulfilled if they were fully backed by a political party. The pattern of socialization of girls and social norms also partly accounted for women's low political participation based on the paradigm of the public and private dichotomy. Many women are deterred from active participation in politics due to the threats of violence and character assassinations which are on the rise. The argument that domestic duties prevented them from participation is commonly voiced by women.

In the specific case of the Naga women, the factors that constrained them from participating in active politics were wide-ranging in nature of which the major ones are discussed in the following section.

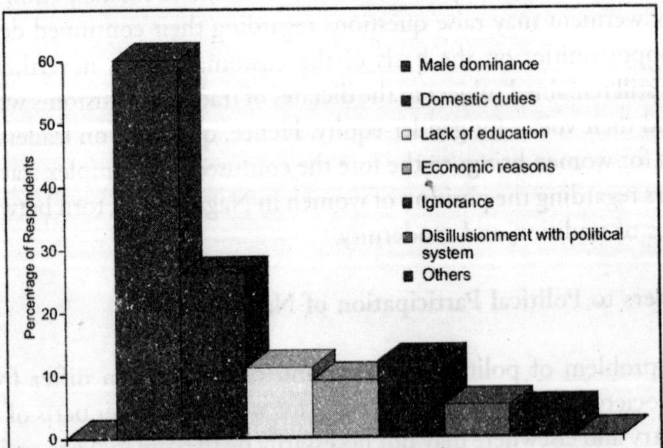

Fig. 5.7: Reasons for Low Political Participation of Naga Women

Male dominance in Naga society figured pre-eminently as the major factor for the low political participation of women. Sixty per cent of the women regard male dominance in Naga society as the primary reason that inhibits the political participation of women. This factor can very well be associated with the patriarchal nature of Naga society, exacerbated by the traditional political system that marginalized women from every aspect of decision-making institutions and out of the domain of public governance. Denied a voice in the political institutions and administration of society, to this day, women in Naga society generally tended to shy away even from the modern political processes, accepting it as the conventional norm of Naga social life. This obviously leaves a clear field for the men in Naga society to continue their political hegemony and have the benefit of running the political and public administration. Many sections of Naga society could not conceive nor accept the idea of having women in leadership roles. This was explicitly borne out of interviews with male elders of the community who were steadfast in their view that men should continue to retain the superior position in society. Further, with regard to the present political process in the State, many women political workers, some of whom had been serving in the same political party for years, opined that though most of the ground works during elections were performed by the women activists, yet, they were never given the due recognition. As a matter of fact, it emerged that even if there were capable women willing to stand for elections, their male counterparts were not willing to neither make way nor give them the opportunity of contesting elections on the party ticket.

Therefore, what becomes apparent is that the traditional mode of governance had been simply carried over and juxtaposed to the modern democratic political system without much alteration in spite of constitutional provisions for equal participation for all irrespective of sex. This is a clear indication that traditional forces over-ride the modern democratic values of equal participation in many societies like that of the Naga society where male hegemony over politics continues to persevere backed by the customary laws.

Besides male dominance, pressures of domestic duties were cited by about a quarter of the women as the reason for the low political participation of Naga women. In this regard it is pertinent to point out that woman in Naga society shoulder a major share of the domestic responsibilities. Many writers had referred to it as an indication of the high status that women enjoy in the society. For instance, in the words of Haimendorf: "Many women in more civilized parts of India may well envy the women of the Naga Hills their high social status....[15] Such Anthropological observations had sometimes been interpreted literally by people ignoring the fact that it was made almost six decades back from a narrow perspective, not from the contemporary point of view. On closer analysis one can see that the much touted freedom in the domestic sphere necessarily entailed more responsibilities than rights. Traditionally, women were required to stay near the homestead, confined to their housework besides bearing and caring for the young. They were expected to contribute to the betterment of the economic position of the household through their work in the fields, weaving and rearing of domestic animals. Should the household prosper the tribute 'naturally' went to the man of the house, but if the household should suffer adversities the blame would inevitably fall on the wife on grounds of 'mismanagement' of household affairs. Even today, in spite of the increasing engagement of Naga women in different professions, the onus of bearing the household responsibilities is still borne largely by them. Consequently it did not allow them with much scope to engage in political activities which understandably demanded long hours and hence very time-consuming. The age old norms and conventions of gender-stereotype, therefore, played a major role in inhibiting the Naga women from more active political role in society.

Naga women's low political participation was also attributed to economic constraints. This aspect was especially significant for those aspiring to run for political office as a candidate. 'Money-power' in the Naga electoral processes remains one of the leading factors for winning an election with 'the exchange of money for votes' being a common-place occurrence during elections in the State. Most women candidates faced the problem of mobilizing resources for use in the elections. Added to this, political parties were often reluctant to field women candidates leaving many with no option but to contest as independents. Banking agencies were not forthcoming with loans to most women since traditionally they do not have access to and control over immovable properties like land which were often required as collateral by the banks to back their loans. This problem basically stemmed from the customary laws of inheritance that denied Naga women a share in the ancestral properties, namely in the form of valuable land and other immovable properties. Till date, many Naga families are not willing to sponsor a female relative as an electoral candidate even if they had the means, while they would do so for a male relative. Such instances reflected the conservative nature of Naga society which viewed males as a more valuable asset to the family, whereas women were seen in the light of a responsibility to be borne by the family.

Lack of education and ignorance were other important factors that emerged as being responsible for the low political participation of women in Naga society which may be considered as an obvious outcome of the socialization process of girls in the society. Though Naga women can be counted amongst one of the most educated lot in the country as far as literacy rates goes, they lacked the political education that is such a vital aspect of socialization. Women were never reckoned in political discussions in the household nor in public, and most often than not, they were socialized and trained to take up the mantle of mistress of the house and the consequential domestic responsibilities. They were effectively conditioned into the stereotype gender role which excluded them from anything political. As a result of being excluded from matters of traditional policy-making, women in Naga society remained ignorant about many important matters in regard to governance of society.

Disillusionment with the prevailing political system was perceived to be yet another deterrent factor responsible for the low political participation of Naga women by a few women. The political process in Nagaland as mentioned elsewhere is perceived to be tainted with corruption, nepotism and use of malpractices at all levels. The politicians in the State were viewed with suspicion and unease, because the image of politics itself was so negative. The electoral processes were characterized by money-power, muscle-power and violence. Given all the negativity associated with the political processes in the State, it gave rise to a sense of disillusionment in a large section of women which kept them away from politics.

Previous results and disinterest in politics were also evinced to be reasons for non-participation among a few women. Previous results, as the reason for low participation of Naga women in politics is self-explanatory. Right from the first General Assembly Elections to the State Legislature in 1964 till 2008, though there had been thirteen women candidates, none of them were elected to office. These results discouraged many Naga women from actively participating in politics, seeing it as a field that had no future for them. As was evident from an analysis of election records, more often than not, women candidates were fielded in those constituencies where the party position was shaky with no obvious chance of winning. As a consequence, women candidates were never able to successfully contest any seat in the State legislature. Naga society was apparently yet to accept women in leadership roles as was reflected in their failure to elect any women to political office till date. Furthermore, going by the voting behaviour, women almost always voted in accordance with the decision of the male family members which worked against the women candidates. The repeated failure of the women candidates had indeed proved very disheartening for women in general and in particular discouraged many aspiring women who otherwise had healthy interest in politics.

The forgoing discussion brings to light that the reasons for the low political participation of Naga women are diverse and complex in character. They face multiple forms of barriers to their political participation which were all culturally determined. The constraints encountered in the path of meaningful political participation came across in various forms which defy a simple answer and solution. However, underlying the different facets of problems was the ever ominous presence and significance of patriarchy and its related characteristics which accounted for many of the obvious extrapolation of Naga women's political and social woes.

REFERENCES

1. Tripathy Swarnamayee, *Political Participation of Women Workers in India*, New Delhi, 2000, p. 9.
2. Andal, N, *Women and Indian Society*, Jaipur, 2002, p. 89.

3. Dahl R., *Who Governs?*, New Haven, 1981.
4. Tripathy Swarnamayee, no.1.
5. *International Encyclopaedia of Sociology*, Vol 2, London, 1995, p. 964.
6. Quoting a Respondent in the present study.
7. Ghadially, Rehana (ed.), *Women in Indian Society*, New Delhi, 1988, p. 18.
8. Noris, Pippa, J. Lovenduski and R. Campbell, *Women's Political Participation in the UK*, 2005. (http://www.electoralcommission.org.uk/) accessed on 5th November, 2006.
9. Gariyali, C.K; Inching Forward: *Political Empowerment of Women in Commonwealth Countries*, New Delhi, 1999, p. 167.
10. *Ibid.*, p. 166.
11. Varma, Sudhir, *Women's Struggle for Political Space*, Jaipur, 1997, p. 134.
12. Ramaswamy, Sushila, Women's Human Rights: A Global Perspective, *Nagaland Post*, June 23, 2000.
13. Mrs. Adangla, Member of AICC, Nagaland unit, interviewed on 3rd October, 2005.
14. This is the case in the Mokokchung Ao Baptist Church, according to the Associate Pastor, Ms. Amenla.
15. Haimendorf, von Christoph, *The Naked Nagas*, London, p. 101.

6

Naga Women and Contemporary Political Issues

The liberal democratic system holds that inequalities can be dealt with by eradicating discriminatory practices through legislation or affirmative action, and that gender relations is central to the strategy of transformative politics. Formal equality for women is unambiguously enshrined within international as well as national law. For instance, Article 5 of the UN Convention on Elimination of All Forms of Discrimination Against Women (CEDAW) hold governments responsible for taking steps to modify practices based on stereotypes about women's role as well as beliefs about women's inferiority.[1] With the grant of formal gender equality, came legal support through a series of legislations. In the Indian context, Article 14 of the Constitution guarantees equality before the law and equal protection under the law. Further, Article 15 prohibits discrimination on ground of religion, race, caste, sex and place of birth.[2] The Constitution has made provision to prohibit traffic in human beings and to provide for just and humane conditions of work along with maternity relief (Article 23 and 42). It is a constitutional duty of every citizen to renounce practices derogatory to the dignity of women (Article 51A). Again Article 16 (1) guarantees equality of opportunity for all citizens in matters relating to employment or appointment to any office under the State. Moreover, the Constitution of India empowered the State to make special provisions for women and children. Further, Legislations like the Equal

Remuneration Act, The Maternity Benefit Act, The Child Marriage Restraint Act, besides a host of other progressive legislations, are some important measures that were implemented to pave way for women to march in step with men. The National Perspective plan for women 1988-2000 is a comprehensive document for their upliftment.

It is noted that though most nations of the world have laws guaranteeing equality to women in all aspects, experience has shown that their participation is likely to remain poor until special efforts are made to ensure their inclusion. Regardless of the fact that the framers of the Constitution of India sought to provide equality to both men and women, it appears the notion of equality was based on gender neutrality and not gender equity. It did not increase the power potential of women so that they could uphold women's well-being. There was no provision to check the imbalance in the social and economic spheres between men and women or to correct centuries old patriarchal attitudes and the resultant lower status of women in societies like the Nagas. With a role in the mainstream denied to them by the male politicians and planners, women could not play any effective role in the mainstream of public life in the country where the odds against them were much more.[3] In the early 1970s, the Committee on the Status of Women in India (CSWI) noted women's ability to produce an impact on the political process has been negligible because of the inadequate attention paid to their political education and mobilization by both political parties and women's organizations. Reviewing women's participation in the political process, the CSWI concluded that: "Though women constituted a numerical majority, they were acquiring the features of a minority group because of an inequality of status and power".[4] The report stressed the need for improving the political status of women as a most important element of the overall problem of socio-economic and political change.

In a State like Nagaland where the political participation of the women remains dismally low, the above given observation of the CSWI holds special significance. For, notwithstanding the various legislations under the Constitution of the country, social codes in Naga society were more often than not determined by the customary laws. For instance, cases of divorce or inheritance were always settled according to customary law which was almost always to the disadvantage of women. But should a woman be dissatisfied with the verdict, theoretically she is at liberty as a citizen of the country to appeal or seek refuge in the statutory laws under the Constitution of India. Naga women were, however, very reticent when it came to taking their case beyond the customary precinct because the traditional jurisdiction was an accepted fact in Naga society. Other factors that inhibited them on this issue were poor economic situation, lack of sufficient knowledge, considerations of modesty, lack of familial support for the same, etc. Women in Naga society holds the view that the existing legislations were not adequate to help women come up on par with their male counterparts because on most matters of dispute in regard to gender relations, recourse is invariably sought in customary law which enjoys special constitutional protection. Article 371 (A) was meant to protect the social and cultural identity of the Nagas. However, the same has provided a pretext to suppress and stifle the Naga women whereby customary law has been used as a convenient instrument to deny women their rights. The women's role in decision-making is effectively blocked by customs that give power to men, which many justify as 'tradition and culture'. As a result, women in Naga society have little skill or experience on matters regarding the administration of the society. Such being the gravity of the political and social predicament of the women in the State, the most viable recourse would be to seek affirmative action.

Affirmative Action represents a strategy to redress previous injustices of racism and sexism in the name of the right of individuals who have suffered to claim their just share of the benefits of individualism, from which they had been excluded.[5] Affirmative action programmes, therefore, help to assure women to positions for which they are qualified, but from which they had been excluded because of systematic discrimination. In India, affirmative action programme by way of Reservation Policy for women has been on offer by many political parties. The Government of India in its National Perspective Plan 1988-2000 recommended reservation for women at all the three tiers of government—national, State and local. Accordingly, the Government of India has, through the Constitutional 73rd Amendment Act 1992, provided 30 per cent reservation for women in the local level of governance, i.e., the Panchayati Raj and the Municipal Councils.

Nagaland being a predominantly tribal society had their own local traditional self-governing institution in the form of village councils at each village which were sovereign entities by all accounts within their jurisdiction. Therefore, the need to implement the Panchayati Raj system of local administration in the State was not deemed necessary. Urban areas were administrated through the Town Committees which gave way to Municipal Councils through the Nagaland Municipal Act 2001. However, this Act predictably did not take cognizance of the provisions under the 73rd Constitutional Amendment Act which provided for one-third reservation for women at the local administrative bodies. After much lobbying by concerned Non-Governmental Organisations (NGOs) and women groups in the State, the provision for one-third reservation for women at the Municipal Councils was finally incorporated into the legislation through the Nagaland Municipal (Amendment) Act 2006. While this move was welcomed by women's organizations across the State, it also opened a Pandora's box in the State with certain section of Naga society, mostly men, vociferously opposed to its implementation. Whereas Nagas have always taken pride in declaring themselves an egalitarian society, yet, the manner in which the thirty-three per cent reservation was being opposed proved their claim a fallacy. Those opposed to this Act cited traditional reasons for their opposition, going so far as to say that women's reservation went against the traditional ethics and norms of governance among the Nagas, that it is a 'murder of democracy'[6], etc. Once the State government gave the green signal for the legislation to be implemented, the panic button appeared to be pushed amongst many men, particularly the existing Municipal Councillors of the State. With almost all the major political parties in the State mouthing support for the said legislation, it was left to some lesser known socio-cultural organizations, with the tacit support of the existing municipal councillors, to voice their resentment and opposition to the Act. The antagonism against the policy went to such an extent that elections to the Mokokchung town municipal council, which was supposed to go to the polls in 2008 could not be conducted and was indefinitely differed amidst strident demands for the deletion of the reservation provision for women. The opposing forces against the policy went public when Municipal Councillors along with several like-minded organisations gave a joint declaration on August 2008 wherein they resolved to demand for scrapping of the reservation for women. The reasons proffered for the resistance ranged from insulting to silly to presumptuous which can be clearly seen in the resolution against the reservation where it stated that the reservation was against customary laws, it would cause more divorces in society, it would lead to more corruption and that it would lead to more law and order problems. Somehow, all this brought to the fore the prevailing confused perceptions regarding the traditional and the modern institutions and the subordinated status of women therein. Even though Municipal Councils are urban civic institutions, the idea of making way for women even within such an urban body could not be conceded to and accepted by some sections of the Naga society considering it to be against the traditional norms of governance as such that existed in the villages.

Those opposed to the legislation failed to reason that with regard to the Nagaland Municipal and town elections, it is electoral voting and such politics itself have never been a part of Naga custom and tradition. However, it is to be said that Nagas, like many other indigenous communities have managed to incorporate key elements and principles of traditional decision making into the modern electoral systems, thus maintaining important aspects of traditional decision-making process such as exclusion of women, within the contemporary political structures. The State government, in spite of the unison of female voices cutting across different tribal organizations and party lines in support of the affirmative policy, ultimately gave in to the opposing forces of the reservation policy and, pointing to their lack of political will, decided to shelve its implementation and instead referred it to a committee to 'study the matter further'[7].

The State government's lackadaisical attitude towards amelioration of women's status can be seen in other instances too. For instance, the State Level Working Committee on Women's Empowerment has asked that a minimum of one-third women be made mandatory in the Village Councils, Village Development Boards, women 'Dobashis'[8], Municipal Boards, Nagaland Public Service Commission and all other recruitment boards.[9] Further, in the State Draft Policy on Empowerment of Women 2003 which was declared after extensive and broad-based consultations, we see some important recommendations, such as—

- Setting up of a State Commission for women to promote the interest of women.
- Provision of financial resources for training and advocacy for women's participation at all levels of decision-making process.
- Changes in personal laws related to marriage, divorce, maintenance, inheritance, guardianship, etc., to eliminate discrimination against women.
- Quota for girls in institutions of higher and technical education.
- Encouraging women to participate in developmental process by providing support services like child care facilities at work places, homes for short stay and free legal aid, to name a few.[10]

This draft policy aimed to bring about advancement and empowerment of women. Almost seven years have lapsed since these recommendations were drafted and except for the setting up of the State Commission for Women nothing else has been done about the recommendations. Even with regard to the State Commission for Women, in the absence of punitive powers, there is every possibility that they may end up functioning like nothing more than a post office. What can be discerned from this lack of inertia on the part of the State government to act upon the policy recommendations is that they simply do not possess the political will needed to see through these measures. In the absence of women in the State assembly to push for women-friendly legislations the situation would most likely continue in the same way, much to the detriment of women's quest for empowerment.

In the midst of the mounting antagonism and resistance targetted against the reservation of women even at the local civic body level, it is with a sense of trepidation that the Naga women are awaiting the draw of the final curtain on the 81st Amendment to the Constitution Bill (Women's Reservation Bill 1996) providing for one-third reservation of seats for women at the State and central legislatures. The debates about the validity of positive discrimination in favour of women at the State and Central Government have raged on for quite some time. There is general disagreement within the ranks of political parties, and even within the women's movement, there is ideological divide on the issue of reservation. While opponents to the policy question whether such affirmative action would indeed bring about a redistribution of power and resources, its proponents argue that greater numerical representation of women in national and State assemblies is the most obvious entry point, and the condition necessary to move towards women's political equality.

Caught up as it were in a myriad of debates, Women's Reservation Bill is eagerly anticipated and enjoys wide support from the women of the State as can be seen in the figure below. Seventy-two per cent of Naga women are in favour of reservation, with just twenty-three per cent saying no to the policy.

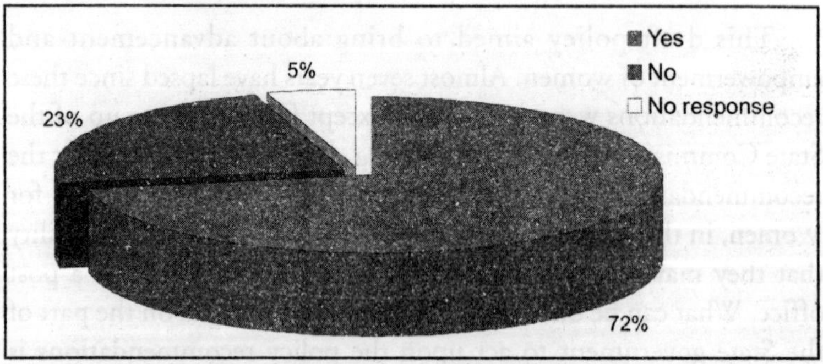

Fig. 6.1: Naga Women's View on the Reservation Policy

There can be observed little difference of opinion on the subject of the policy of reservation between the rural and the urban women with almost an equal percentage of both approving the said policy. The general sentiment prevalent amongst those women in favour of the reservation policy appeared to be that because of widespread incidence of gender bias against female leadership in Naga society, reservation is deemed necessary in order to provide women an opportunity to prove their capabilities. The society being male dominated, unless special measures like the reservation policy were implemented in its proper perspective, Naga women would never be able to push through the male ranks of politicians. Moreover, Naga women lacked the confidence and their social conditioning of being on the fringe-line of politics prevented them from coming to the fore of political arena. Therefore, numerical strength in the parliament and State legislatures was seen as crucial for the women to create a springboard to deal concertedly with issues that concern them. Many Naga women, however, had a word of caution regarding the duration of the policy. The general opinion was that the Reservation policy should be enforced only for a certain time period, and not on a permanent basis. It was felt that the policy was required only to kick off women into mainstream decision-making bodies, to create a foothold to discharge their civic responsibilities as equal citizens second to none. This would create conditions whereby Naga women could come forward boldly and be part of the governing system. There exists a strong feeling amongst the women for the need to be part of the governing institutions seeing it as the means to address more effectively issues that impacts upon them as women and as concerned citizens of their society. A handful of Naga women were opposed to the reservation policy on the ground that women were equally competent and educated as men and hence could very well do without reservation. This opinion appeared to be mere idealism against the larger picture of the structural obstacles faced by Naga women. Those women who were against the policy felt that reservation would portray a negative image of women because it appeared to be nothing short of asking for special consideration which would tantamount to conceding that women were not capable enough to stand on their own feet. They opined that if women were really determined, they should be able to prove themselves without falling back on the reservation policy which they regard as gender-condescending. They were not willing to depend on the 'concessions' given out on account of their gender.

Therefore, we see two very different points of view with their own set of justifications and reasoning. The scale tilts in favour of the reservation policy, which seemed to echo the common feeling of most Naga women today. Many women in the State have realized that without some sort of policy of affirmative action, they had indeed no hope of breaking through the male ranks of male politicians who were not prepared to make way for or accommodate women within their parties as well as in the legislature. This attitude in fact blends well with the patriarchal social structure of the Nagas which provided absolutely no space for women in the political sphere of the traditional governance that operated in the villages—the core of Naga society.

Naga society is basically a village society. More than eighty-two per cent[11] of the Naga population still lives in villages. Every Naga, including the urban dwellers, traced their ancestral roots back to their respective villages. Irrespective of their socio-economic standing a Naga without proper or uncertain ancestry always had a dubious identity. People viewed them with suspicion. Hence, for every single Naga the village played an integral role in their life, regardless of the modern facade of the towns. Within every village, the Village Council is the administrative seat which was the highest decision-making body in the villages since time immemorial. Every major decision concerning the administration of the villages are borne by the Village Council. Any disputes within the village jurisdiction were settled by the Village Council. They are in every way the legally recognized custodians of customary laws and usages. The most striking aspect of the Village Council in this modern era is the absence of women members. It continues to be exclusively a male preserve. The Village Area and Council Act 1978 (Amended in 1985, 1990), is a village based administration system developed upon traditional institutions of the Nagas, on the basis of customary laws and procedures. According to the Act, 'A Village Council shall consist of members, chosen by villagers in accordance with the prevailing customary practices and usages, the same being approved by the State Government....'[12] Thus, though the Act was relatively recent, it merely reaffirmed the age old existing systems of governance and remained silent on the issue of women's role in the Village Councils and inclusion in governance.

The only singular provision which allowed for Naga women to be part of the developmental activities is through the Village

Development Board (VDB) in the village, governed under the Village Development Model Rules 1980. The VDB of Nagaland is a unique rural planning and development institution which is based on the rich traditional heritage of the community life of the Nagas. It emerged from the widely acknowledged fact today that development planning needs to be decentralized in order to involve people in the planning process, to formulate plans as per the local needs. The concept of decentralized planning has gained momentum as it has been increasingly felt that the 'top-down approach' has not succeeded in meeting the aspirations of people at the grass root level. Hence, taking advantage of the favourable socio-cultural state of affairs in Naga society the Government of Nagaland formally launched the VDB in the State under Clause 12 of Section 12 of the Nagaland Village and Area Council Act 1978. The primary objective of the VDB is to effectively channelize development to the Villages through grass root level planning and implementation of the programmes and projects. It was done so with a view to achieve the ideals of removal of rural poverty through community asset building and employment generation. It also aimed to ensure the devolution of economic power to the rural mass with the noble intention of raising the standard of living and to bridge the emerging gap of social disparity through economic enlistment. Involving the villagers in the State developmental affairs through recognition of the traditional system of governance in Nagaland was also another objective of the Act.

The VDBs function under the directives of the Village Councils. According to the VDB Model Rules, under Article 4 (B), it states, "The number of women members to be included in the Management Committee of the VDB should not be less than one-fourth of the total number of members of the Management of the VBDs".[13] Women were allotted twenty-five per cent of the funds from the Grant-in-aid that comes for the village development. This fund was meant to be used for the welfare and developmental schemes of the village women. Officially, it is mandatory for the VDB to submit the names of just two women member to the concerned department. Accordingly, each village has worked out their own modalities of appointing women members. Therefore, while some villages in Nagaland have as many as nineteen women VDB members, the number of women VDB members in other villages ranges from two to seven.

Women VDB members were required to implement and monitor schemes for women in coordination with the general VDB. They also organize seminars and meetings occasionally, and assist the general VDB in all developmental works. But a sense of discontentment could be discerned amongst the women in the Village Development Boards many of whom strongly opined that a change from the present system of operation was required. When queried on the nature of alteration they were vying for, the unanimous view emerged that they wanted change by way of enhancement in their powers and functions. Women members in most VDBs felt constraint and as such powerless to usher in much required changes, because, as per their accounts, under the present system the women VDB members did not have the autonomy to function independently. Everything they did was subject to the approval of the general male dominated VDB and the Village Councils.

In addition to such a constraint, women VDB members across the State agreed that the present fund allocation system for women was not adequate to meet their needs and objectives. In fact, with regard to the allocation of one-fourth of the total VDB fund for women's developmental projects, it was established that in many villages the male VDB members were not willing to part with that fund and hand it over to their women counterparts. They would like to see a review in the funding system aimed at its enhancement. Many women VDB members strongly opined that given the opportunity and the adequate financial assistance, they had the latent ability to do so much more at present, and effectively too. It may be noted that, the potential of Naga women in implementing development projects effectively and judiciously, has gained recognition by the Department of Rural Development in Nagaland, which stated that: "To ensure utilization of fund with proper implementation of schemes, more projects should be given to the women committees under Rural Development".[14] Consequent upon the satisfactory performance of women VDB cells in many villages, there was also a proposal that a sub-committee for women should be constituted in VDB to facilitate more women participation in village developmental work.[15] However, till date the involvement of women is confined only to the development schemes of women, and they do not have much say in the broader male dominated VDB. Moreover, the functioning of the VDB is subject to the approval of the Village Council, where again there was no female representation. Hence, the role of the women VDB members in the governance of the villages remains limited as in the face of various constraints they were not in a position to influence the policy decisions. Besides the implementation of certain fund-raising schemes for women's welfare within the allotted fund, they could not play any significant role in the administration and governance of the village. The present system being followed where formal nomination of only two women members in the VDB by the Village Council was required often becomes mere tokenism. Due to lack of numerical strength they were in no position to influence the policy decisions of the VDB. Therefore, in order to ensure representation of women in critical numbers, the effective implementation of VDB Act is imperative. Women representation in the VDB needs to be made proportional to their population.

Besides the lack of numerical strength, the ignorance of women about their due rights even with regard to the functioning of the VDB system is another major hindrance to the realization of goals of economic empowerment. Women in many villages were blissfully unaware of the fact that they were, as a social category entitled to one-fourth of the VDB fund for their developmental scheme and were quite content to follow the lead of their male counterparts. This resulted in the fraudulent use of the VDB funds in many villages. Therefore, awareness generation and education of the women with regard to their rights is a necessary step which should be undertaken without delay. This will ensure fairer decentralization of developmental governance at grass root level which would go a long way in boosting the morale of the Naga women and enhancing their skill and confidence.

With the literacy rate of Naga women showing very positive trends, many girls and women are opting to pursue higher education and a career. Being increasingly exposed to modern ideas and concepts, they were bound to view the existing state of affairs regarding barring of women from the traditional decision-making bodies of society with new eyes. And indeed, today's Naga women were concerned with ushering in changes in the traditional mode of governance. A State level survey on this issue shows that seventy-two per cent of the Naga women held the view that women's role as citizens should be recognized and, therefore, they should be duly included in the Village Councils and be made an integral part of the governance process.[16]

The following possible modes of inclusion for women in the Village Councils could be considered:

- Village Council and Area Act 1978 should be amended and seats should be created for women representatives. It should be amended to harmonize with constitutional provisions and international obligations.
- Through nomination by other women. Women could be nominated into the Village Council by the women themselves, so that there would be a fair representation of both the sexes in the traditional decision-making institution.
- Nomination of women members as clan representatives of each clan.
- Nomination according to male-female ratio.
- Through reservation. Many women were of the view that at the initial stage, there was a need for reservation of seats even in the Village Council. Such a policy would effectively serve to break the conventional norm of governance at the local level, thereby, creating a space for Naga women in the grass root governance of their own society.

Naga women in general concur that they ought to be given the opportunity of equal partnership in all matters of management of the village. A definite opinion amongst women in Nagaland was that gaining membership into the Village Council is a prerequisite to fight for property rights of women who, as per Naga custom were denied the right to inherit parental property. As in the case of other issues concerning women, the female voices of the rural women resonates equally to that of the urban women. So basically, the awakening of women's rights consciousness cuts across rural-urban differences in Naga society.

REFERENCES

1. Chatterjee, Mohini, *Women's Human Rights*, Jaipur, Aavishkar Publishers, 2005, p. 86.
2. Menon, Nivedita (ed.), *Gender and Politics in India*, 1999, New Delhi, p. 201.
3. Sharma, Kumud, *Transformative Politics: Dimensions of Women's Participation in Panchayati Raj*, New Delhi, p. 23.
4. *Ibid.*, p. 26.
5. Subhasini, Mahapatra, *Women and Politics*, New Delhi, 2001, p. 17.
6. The State government of Nagaland called a Consultative Meet on 8th October, 2010 to discuss matters related to the Women's reservation in Municipal bodies besides some other issues. Despite eloquent arguments by women bodies on the need for reservation, tribal civil society bodies primarily male organisations stood up against the policy on various grounds as mentioned. They were more in favour of nomination of women into the civic bodies fully conscious of the fact that nominated members would not have voting rights. The Consultative meet did not result in a conclusive decision much against the wishes of the women representatives who were vying for a decision in favour of the reservation policy.
7. The municipal elections which were supposed to be held in 2008 could not be conducted due to the opposition against the reservation of thirty-three per cent seats for women in the civic body. Instead of implementing the policy as per law, the State government instead constituted a committee to study the matter further.
8. 'Dobashi' (*do-basha*) literally means 'two-language'. They were basically people engaged as interpreters by the British administrators in their interaction with the local communities. After independence of the country the role of *dobashis* got institutionalized under the new administrative system and they continued functioning as intermediaries between the local people and the political officers

(administrators). In the process their powers and functions expanded resulting in the institutionalization of *dobashi*-courts, set up to settle cases and disputes on the basis of customary laws. Hence, today, as interpreters of customary law and practices, they enjoy judicial powers too. *Dobashis* have remained a male domain over the years. With growing awareness and debate on women's rights issues in contemporary times, *dobashi*-courts are perceived to be gender-biased against women as most customary laws are deemed discriminatory towards women. Hence, the call for women to be inducted as *dobashis* in recent times has been growing.

9. Nagaland State Human Development Report 2004, Government of Nagaland.
10. *Ibid.*
11. Directorate of Economics and Statistics, Government of Nagaland, Kohima, 2001.
12. The Nagaland Village and Area Councils Act 1978, Government of Nagaland, Kohima, 1979.
13. Village Development Model Rules 1980 (Revised), Government of Nagaland, Department of Rural Development, 1997.
14. "Policy and Strategy of Rural Development Programmes in Nagaland", (Department of Rural Development, Nagaland, 1995).
15. *Ibid.*
16. Jamir, Toshimenla, '*Political Consciousness and Participation of Naga Women: A Sociological Enquiry*' (Ph.D Thesis), Nagaland University 2007.

7
Conclusion

The principal world body, the United Nations Organization, in its historic Millennium Summit in 2000 where one hundred and fifty Heads of State Governments gathered at New York, arrived to a conclusion and declared that the only possible measure to combat poverty, hunger and disease, and also to stimulate development that is truly sustainable, is through empowering women folks around the world. This UN declaration bears significance because, indirectly or directly, it is asserting that perception of women as second class citizens of the soil were totally wrong and also an indication of the dawning cognizance that the world cannot go ahead without women's participation in all human aspects. Gender equality in various forms of political participation, therefore, assumes importance as the liberation of women from subordination is essentially a political task which can be accomplished when women become a political force. The most vital dimensions of political participation in a democracy are voting, contesting in elections, campaigning and political membership. These four dimensions form the basis for basic participation in public affairs by the citizens. To utilize these given democratic rights in a proper perspective requires political socialization. Judicious usage of these rights, lead to a stable political system and a fair and legal system.

In the context of the Naga Society it is worth noting that the cultural practice of gender marginalization from decision-making bodies have impacted negatively on the political socialization of women with the consequence that even after more than fifty years of modern democratic electoral system, no woman have succeeded in making entry into the hallowed portals of the State Assembly. While modern education and related developments are gradually awakening a feminist consciousness amongst many Naga women who are trying to work for meaningful change, the goal remains elusive in the face of patriarchal obstacles. While there have been slogans for the rights and freedom for the women in Nagaland, and the upper educated strata of Naga society abounds with evidence of modernization and apparent sense of equality, a closer inspection of this professed equality presents a different reality. For, despite the superficial veneer of egalitarianism, there is almost no participation of women in decision making, whether at the village, district or State level. It is clear that gender-specific values have emerged in contemporary Naga society. This includes the notion that Naga women and men are intrinsically unequal, that men have certain roles and women others, and that politics is the realm of Naga men, not women. Such perceptions have unfortunately taken a firm hold in Naga society, very often at the expense of the women.

A close analysis into the pattern of political participation of women in Naga society brings to light the sociological factors that effortlessly weave within and through the complex realms of their besieged political life. Modern political system, particularly the electoral process, has, instead of closing the gender gap in governance, served to further widen the bridge between men and women in Naga society, thereby bringing into sharp focus the gender inequality that exists in society. Paradoxical though it may seem, the lot of Naga women has changed for the better and yet things have remained the same, as a result of the women's movement. Rationale may be found in the fact that Naga women have lived in two types of reality—the legal and the social. Liberal thinkers in the country have tried to amend archaic and sexiest laws derogatory to women through progressive legislations. Hence, being a part of the national citizenry, the legal reality has been moving in a progressive and sanguine direction. However, the psychological and social realities in which Naga women live have remained virtually unchanged. The myths, customs and values that shape Naga people's perception of and attitude toward women are too fossilized for any significant dent to be made to transform their lives for the better. On the other hand, as a result of the women's movement and the subsequent related literature and education women in Naga society are awakening to the harsh realities that they had all along been deprived of their political rights in the name of tradition and custom.

The emerging perceptions of the Naga women are forward looking and their political consciousness and awareness is appreciably positive. However, this awareness has not been transformed into political action on the part of the women. Their political participation exhibits an asymmetrical picture, particularly when we juxtapose their high level of voting with other facets of political participation such as political membership, campaign or contesting. No doubt, one of the most important components of political participation in a democracy is the exercise of one's franchise. The trend of voting among the female electorate in Nagaland indicated that in no way do Naga women lag behind men as far as voting is concerned. In fact, in the years 1987 and 1989, the number of women voters surpassed those of the men in the State General Elections with 85.9 per cent and 86 per cent of female votes as against 83.2 per cent and 85.3 per cent of make votes respectively. In spite of the large turnout of women voters, it is noteworthy that not a single woman candidate who have contested so far in the General Elections between 1964 up to 2008, were ever elected to the State Legislature. The Naga electorate obviously does not vote in favour of the women candidates. The lack of support and empathy for women candidates do not reflect the incapability of the candidates themselves but is in fact symptomatic of other cultural constraints that stand in the way of the women candidates. One of such constraints can be traced to the important determinants of voting behaviour of the Naga electorate which includes considerations of kinship ties, economic considerations, and political affinity of family members, and rarely rests on political ideology, issues or party principles. In the case of some women, voting is motivated by poverty. Again for many, the choice of candidate depended on the decision of the male members in the family. As most men in Naga society were biased against female leadership, it does adversely affect the outcome of the women candidates in the elections.

It is significant that though women constitute 47.61 per cent of the population in Nagaland (2001 Census), the number of women candidates had never reached even two per cent of the total candidature. An analysis of the pattern of candidature of the women candidates in Nagaland revealed that their candidature was often not backed by any political parties. For instance, a look at their candidature from 1987 to 2003 shows that out of the seven women candidates, four of them (fifty-seven per cent) contested as Independent candidates. This highlights the disinclination of the political parties in the State to field women candidates in the elections. With money playing a primary role in the electoral processes in Nagaland, the chances of winning the elections for a woman candidate becomes next to impossible without the backing and financial support of a political party. Indeed a very important deterrent to women's active participation as candidates was the increasing expense of elections. A probable factor for the lack of support of the political parties for women's candidature can be linked to the dismally low level of political membership of women in the party organizations. Political parties are the most common route to elected office. They play a decisive role in determining the prospects for any women aspiring to public office. Since political parties are considered to be the main vehicles to increase women's mobilization and are important tools of political empowerment, lack of political membership of the Naga women works to their disadvantage definitively. When a woman actually entered a political party, she usually struggled against being a side-piece or a doormat because she is considered extraneous to the factors that propel men to power. With women missing from the forefront of the political organizations and parties, they were not accorded due recognition for the efforts they put in, particularly during election times. It is argued that much of the groundwork during the electioneering are actually done by the women. Being in a numerically disadvantaged position women were compelled to simply play foot soldiers of their male colleagues and more seriously, they cannot forge any common agenda within and across the parties for women's upliftment. Even within the party hierarchy, Naga women found it tough to reach the top party position where all policy decisions are taken. For instance in the BJP State working committee, out of twelve members, there was only one woman, in the middle rung of the party hierarchy. Again in the list of the NPCC office bearers, which is the oldest and most organized political party in Nagaland, out of twelve members, there was not a single woman.[1] The gender-scene is no different in the other political parties too. Most of the women political activists in the State are concentrated at the lower levels of the political party structure and, therefore, not in a position to influence any party decision. Thus, decisions regarding the support of women candidature or the fielding of women candidate in the elections are all in the hands of the male politicians. And more often than not, the idea of fielding women candidates is not regarded favourably as exemplified by the low number of women candidates in the State Assembly Elections as per record. Most political parties deny women candidate party tickets on account of their non-win ability factor, which serves to perpetuate male dominance in the political process of the State.

However, it is encouraging to note that currently there are visible signs of efforts by some political parties like the Congress (I) to accommodate more women members within its party hierarchy. In December 1998, the Congress Party amended the Party Constitution by which thirty per cent of all posts in the organization are reserved for women.[2] For many years, though the Women's Wing of the party, The Mahila Congress was in existence, the party leaders never made any effort to promote its members to the national level of the Congress Party, the All India Congress Committee (AICC). However, as per the directive of the central committee there are two women functionaries from the State of Nagaland in the AICC.[3] A most crucial role can be played by the Naga women incumbents in the AICC in helping other women from the State to come up to higher positions. Their role would be critical in so far as they can use their position of power at the national level to press for changes in the State party structure so that more numbers of deserving Naga women can be given due opportunity at leadership in the party. Another significant development which is notable is the appointment of the first Naga woman to the post of Gaon Bura[4] in Dimapur Municipal Council in October 2005. Traditionally, the institution of Gaon Bura (GB) was the sole domain of the men folk. It remains to be seen whether this positive development heralds the beginning of a new trend of Naga women administrators, or would be just a one-time event. If the recent resolution adopted by the GBs Federation of Nagaland holds, wherein they 'prohibited' the appointment of women as GBs, then any future additional appointment of women as Gaon Buras seem highly improbable.[5]

Engagement in electoral campaigns is a very important dimension of political participation. The participation of the Naga women in this aspect of political participation is exceptionally low. Electoral campaigning in the State is often viewed in negative light due to its characterization of criminalization, association with easy money and the excessive use of liquor. Such factors deterred most women from keenly engaging with it. In the absence of democratic spirit and principles from this dimension of political activity it resulted in a very low level of participation by the women.

Education has always been regarded as a propellant for increased political awareness and activity. It emerges, however, that the political participation of Naga women decreases with the rise in their educational level. This invalidates the general assumption that greater degree of political participation is a corollary of higher education, that, the more educated people get the higher level of engagement in political activity. This has been a widespread belief among most social scientists. In respect to voting, membership in political parties, and electoral campaigns, Naga women with low to moderate level of education were found to be the highest participants, while the lowest participants were those with the highest level of education. There is a clear indication that most educated Naga women preferred to keep a good distance from political activities. This unlikely trend among the educated section of women in Nagaland reflected their disillusionment with the prevailing political system in the State which was no longer perceived as a viable instrument to usher in positive changes in society. Naga women were increasingly focusing on other avenues for empowerment, mainly through higher education and economic self-sufficiency. However, it is important to note that the process of empowerment involves not just an improvement in physical and social conditions, but also equal participation in decision-making process, control over resources, and mechanism for sustaining these gains. To attempt to change the social institutions that embody the basic and unequal power structures in society requires active participation by Naga women in the political decision-making machineries.

Towards this end, the educational system, especially the colleges and universities in Nagaland can play a positive role in reversing the trend of declining political participation among educated Naga women. Though campuses cannot be expected to promote political engagements, the educational system can certainly play a crucial role. It can prepare the students of higher education, especially the female students, to become engaged citizens who recognize themselves as members of a larger social fabric and to take action where appropriate. This needs a thorough review of the existing educational system with a special focus on the curriculum and teaching methods. Every effort can be made to eliminate gender-based discriminatory study materials and incorporate in their stead study resources that are gender-sensitive and which promote the principles of egalitarian values and ethics.

Other factors that played a significant role in determining the nature of the political participation of the women in Nagaland was their age and marital status. The political participation of Naga women increases with the increase in their age. This can be termed as the 'bio-social' factor which affects the political participation of women. Naga women in the age group 28-38 years were the least politically active, while the women of age group 48 and above were most involved and active in political activities. This phenomenon in Naga society can be attributed to the trend towards relatively late marriages, normally around 25-30 years of age, as many Naga women were opting to pursue higher education, and subsequently settle into some professional career before marriage. Subsequently women in the age group of 28-38 would, in all probability be fully engaged in child-bearing and rearing, besides their careers, if any. On the other hand, older women were relatively more settled in life, domestically as well as professionally, so they would not get hindered by the bio-social role of reproduction and associated gender roles that were expected of them. Sharing the burden of household responsibilities by the men folk would ease the bio-social constraints of the Naga women to a large extent thereby facilitating more time and energy for political participation. The fact that domestic duties prevented them from participation is commonly voiced by women in urban areas.

The marital status of the women in the State had a significant bearing on their political participation. There are explicit indications that married women were more politically active than unmarried women in Naga society. In fact most of the politically active married women were found to do so under the influence of their husbands. For many of them, their interest in politics developed only after marriage. This accounted for the major reason why political participation is higher among married Naga women. Another important reason for the non-participation of unmarried women in the political processes of the State was the negative image of present day politics in the State. Politics was perceived as an immoral activity. This in itself deterred many young girls from active participation. Young women who were seen to be too active in politics often landed up with tarnished or negative reputation, which in all probability could ruin their marriage prospects. As a result, educated women, as well as unmarried girls, hesitated to get involved in the electoral politics of the State. Marriage, it is observed, serves to provide a 'safe cushion' wherein women no longer had to worry about their reputation and the related consequences in their social life. Hence, marital status constituted a critical factor that affected the political participation among Naga women in a constructive manner. It can be argued on this aspect that unless the electoral process and related activities in Nagaland undergoes a dramatic transformation to clean up its act and become more congruent with ideals of fair democratic system, the participation trend of women may not see much change. In the process, it deprived the Naga society of young and feminine perspective in its political processes.

Despite the widespread belief in the lower political participation of rural women, in all the four vital dimensions of political participation, i.e., voting, political campaign and political membership, the participation of the women from the rural areas were considerably higher than their urban counterparts. This unexpected and rather unusual phenomenon can perhaps best be explained through certain practices that frequently took place in the rural areas during elections. In many Naga villages, it is a common practice for the village council to take the collective decision on behalf of the entire village to support a particular candidate or party. Such decision by the village council, constituted of only males, became binding on all the villagers irrespective of sex or position. Normally, nobody in the village opposed or stood up against such kind of collective decision by the village council since they were the ultimate authority. To deviate from such a dictate would imply inviting the wrath of the entire village. The motive for their collective decision could be based on certain traditional and historical reasons, or it may even be a bargain for certain economic gain, or promises of some developmental work for the village. This resulted in the apparently higher rate of participation of both men and women from the rural areas in the electoral process.

Moreover, considerations of kinship and clan ties were held more seriously and steadfast in the rural areas given the fact that rural areas were by nature, more traditional and conservative. Supporting and voting for a particular candidate on the basis of clan or family ties was also very common. Therefore, political participation of the rural women became part of a community affair, and not necessarily an indication of high political consciousness of the rural Naga women *per se*. Furthermore, women in urban areas were comparatively more educated than the rural women. Therefore, as per the adverse relationship that exists between higher education and political participation of Naga women, perhaps it is only logical that rural women, whose educational levels were much lower, do exhibit relatively higher levels of political participation.

Naga women do not show a strong desire to participate directly in the electoral politics of the state and their political participation is found to be severely inadequate. That is not to say that they have remained outside the political paradigm. They have their own roles, but to a large extent these were limited to playing foot soldiers to political parties and their candidates during elections. After more than four decades of statehood under democratic principles, substantive political participation of Naga women is still absent. The political participation of Naga women apparently seemed confined to mere voting on which aspect there is no gender gap. But in the role of women as candidates, political party membership, and as electoral campaigners, their participation is dismally low and lags far behind men. Though voting is indispensable to representative democracy, unless it is accompanied by the other political activities such as campaigning, political membership, or contesting in elections, it reduces citizenship to a superficial and relatively passive activity. Therefore, the Naga women's mode of political participation in the electoral process of the State can be viewed as a passive form of political participation. As a result, politics in Nagaland remained a male domain in respect of numbers, membership in political parties, position in the party hierarchy, and presence and effectiveness in the State Legislature.

Women in Nagaland have a very low level of confidence regarding their ability to influence the political process of the State. Their low political efficacy adversely affects their political status, compelling many to stay away from the political arena. Most women felt that their participation would not make any difference to the political system which was characterized by corruption and other negative factors anyway. Despite their low political efficacy, most Naga women, political activists as well as lay women were of the opinion that increased political participation of women would positively enhance women's position in Naga society. The reasons forwarded by the women reflected their growing awareness and consciousness regarding their subordinated position in Naga society. They favoured increased participation of women in the political arena seeing it as an avenue to make the views and perspectives of women to be taken into account while framing policies. They opined that only when women were a part of the decision-making institutions, would traditional laws which were discriminatory towards women, such as those relating to matters of property rights, marriage and divorce, would be reviewed and restructured in favour of women. Only then, they felt, women would be in a position where they could break free from traditional dominance of male opinion and decision-making in all spheres of life, and take charge of their own destiny.

Most of the Naga women were of the opinion that they should be given more opportunity in the political arena by the existing political parties. Merely on account of their gender Naga women were unduly deprived of the opportunity to participate as per their capability and potentiality. Many women across the State opined that better policies are essential to really bring women on par with men. As a step towards better political representation of woman, they favoured the policy of reservation of seats which has been on the agenda of several political parties and the Government of India since 1996. The general opinion amongst the women folk is that numerical strength in the Parliament and State Legislature was a prerequisite to make the voices of Naga women be heard concertedly. Given an opportunity, there was every possibility Naga women could perform any task as well if not better than most of their male counterparts, it is opined. Also a rather subjective argument was forwarded that women in the State would probably be less corrupt than men and would be more concerned about social issues, and not be as 'power-crazy' as most men were.

However, despite strong opinions in favour of women candidature and enhanced political participation, Naga women do not possess the political aspiration needed to become politically assertive. This lack of political aspiration among the Naga women runs contrary to their strong approval for more political participation by women. Though most of them personally advocated an enhanced role of women in public governance, when it came to the question of acceptability of the same by the Naga society, one comes across a perplexing picture. Reflecting the complexities of the present Naga society, less than half of the women thought that Naga society is ready to accept women in leadership roles. In spite of the progressive perceptions of the women today, the larger Naga society was not ready to accept women in leadership roles, especially in the arena of public governance. Therefore, the strong desire to see women in leadership roles among the Naga women appears to be confined only at the idealistic level. Perhaps, excluding women from the decision-making process for centuries, right from the village level, has created a sense of alienation and a sense of unworthiness. Such perceptions urgently required a change in the mindset and attitude of the people which could be brought about largely through gender-sensitive education and dissemination of information.

Naga women are not lagging behind in political consciousness or awareness, adding to the many contradictions that characterizes the nature of women's political participation in the State. In fact they are quite well-informed and aware of the issues concerning the State government, for instance. This is amply illustrated through the factors forwarded by them on the basis of which they had evaluated the performance of the State government such as the situation of employment or unemployment for that matter, infrastructural development, transparency in functioning, mismanagement of public funds, accessibility to the public, their stand on the peace process between the Government of India and the Naga national movement, poor management skills, creation of job opportunities, and creation of a new Department for Women Development, to name some major ones. It indicated that the women are knowledgeable enough about social and public issues of governance, having their own strong opinions on the above mentioned issues. Thus, contrary to their low political participation in the electoral process of the State, political consciousness of the Naga women is very high. This in itself does not conform to expected notions about the positive correlation between political consciousness and political participation.

The inability to translate their political consciousness into political action is one of the ambivalences that characterize the contemporary political situation of Naga women. While on the one hand, the level of awareness and eagerness of the Naga women to see changes in the governing system of the present Naga society is quite conspicuous, on the other hand, a perceptible uncertainty and lack of confidence to come forward and plunge into public affairs and governance can be seen. Insight into Naga women's role in the domestic and social sphere may lead to the covert factors responsible for this contradiction. Naga women, even though heavily engaged in a myriad of domestic responsibilities in addition to their professional careers in the case of many, they appeared to be quite contented with their domestic lot and were not actively seeking for a change in the state of affairs. In fact only sixteen per cent of the women interviewed wanted a change in their domestic schedules. Perhaps the fact that women in Naga society enjoyed relative freedom in the domestic sphere accounted for the State of complacency among them to a large extent. For, it is said, as long as the home front runs smoothly men generally did not interfere in the domestic affairs. Individual liberty to choose one's own career as well as life partner was also a given fact in Naga society. In the process it effectively served to null the effects of deprivation imposed by their marginalization in the public sphere and denial of political rights. By giving them a false illusion of egalitarianism on the basis of their position in the domestic sphere, Naga women's inferior status was not identified with specific structural injustices that could be targetted by agitations. Therefore, in spite of the increasing momentum of the women's movement not only in the west but around the globe as well by the end of the nineteenth century, one does not find a comparable interest in rectifying the exclusion of women from public life in Naga society. So well conditioned are they into the patriarchal social structure that the idea of questioning the prevailing norms of male dominance in public life appears not to hold much appeal for them.

The repression of the public role of women in Naga society can, therefore, firmly be associated with male dominance under the institution of patriarchy and related value system. The pre-eminence of male dominance as the primary factor for the low political participation of Naga women can in turn be linked with the traditional political system which had excluded women from every decision-making institution in society, effectively marginalizing them to the periphery of public domain and the private sphere. The traditional political system of male governance somehow was carried over into the modern democratic political system. Even though a new political system had been introduced in Naga society, it was merely superimposed on the pre-existing social system where women were not accorded any place in the governance of society. Unless space is created for Naga women in the traditional seats of decision-making by reviewing and restructuring the customary law to suit the modern era, the possibility of their entry into the modern political institutions of governance appears to be a distant prospect.

The direct consequence of the Naga cultural ethos upon the life processes of women can hence be classified into three categories—social, economic and political consequences. In the social sphere, Naga culture and norms accorded women a respectable position. Naga men were generally very protective about their female family members and concurred respect to them in the social sphere. In the domestic sphere too Naga women enjoyed a high degree of autonomy in running the household with her given role as mistress of the house. The freedom enjoyed by Naga women in the social and domestic spheres provided them with an illusion of egalitarianism, boosted further by prevailing cultural notions of gender equality professed by many tribal societies like the Nagas. Further, most of the literature available on Naga society and its culture were written by male ethnographers from outside the State and some male local writers, who wrote and reflected simply their male perspective of the society and the gender relations therein. In the process, they failed to see the reality of the women's position within the Naga social structure and, hence, projected a not too accurate image of being an egalitarian society. However, present sociological analysis does bring to light many of the cultural deprivations faced by the women solely on the basis of their gender. The false sense of gender-equality derived on the basis of their position in the domestic sphere consequently nullified many of the signs of discrimination and deprivation accorded to Naga women in the political and economic sphere. Their contented position in the domestic sphere subdued the women from raising their voices against the gender injustices in society even while the rest of the world were reverberating under the influence of the women's liberation movement.

The political consequence of the Naga tradition and culture on the women has been their almost total eclipse from the administrative and decision-making bodies and institutions which continue till date. This has deprived many Naga women from acquiring the political skills and knowledge needed for meaningful participation in the political processes. The net effect of this exclusion is the unutilization of valuable female human resource and denial of the feminine perspective on all issues of governance of society. This belies the claims to 'Pure democracy'[6] of the Nagas as spoken of and written about by a number of scholars. When approximately half of the population is excluded from decision-making processes and denied the opportunity to voice their opinions and views, questions of democracy, equality, social justice and human rights come into sharp focus. Democracies require a fair representation of both the sexes and, therefore, claims to true democracy cannot be validated when women are virtually excluded from positions of decision-making and power. Also the legitimacy of an all-male decision-making comes under question in a democratic system. There cannot be equitable resource allocation without the participation of women in representative numbers.

In the economic arena, by denying them the right to inheritance of parental property Naga customary law in effect lowered the economic status of women. The traditional system of male inheritance has led to the growth of male-owned private property, with the family as the institution that appropriates and perpetuates it. The consequence it had on the political participation of Naga women was deleterious for their political empowerment. Pecuniary capability constituted one of the most decisive requisites for political success today where money, more than political ideology or ethics, does the talking for a major bulk of the electorate in Nagaland and elsewhere. A critical re-evaluation of the traditional inheritance system, therefore, has become imperative. For, despite the impressive gains that Naga women has made, there were significant disparities like economic inequality that needed to be addressed if one were to articulate seriously on issues of social justice. A neglected dimension in many studies is effective control of ownership and the use of property. In the Naga society the ownership pattern of house and property was clearly patriarchal with only about five per cent of the women actually able to claim ownership to the house they were living in.[7] Inequality in command over property is considered as the single most important form of persistent economic inequality between women and men. The consequences in its entirety, of the traditional customary law of inheritance in the case of the Naga women was that, most women had less direct independent access than men to capital, property, markets and extension services. Naga women, for instance, had very restricted access to credit because of their lack of collateral in the form of property or other immovable assets. Property not only raised the status of the owner, it can be a direct and indirect means of production; income and subsistence can be derived from it, and also the right to credit, mortgages or subsistence can be gained. Hence, the denial of the right to inheritance of the Naga women and the subsequent lack of control over valuable assets and property not only devalued their worth and standing in society, but in the process deprived them the economic security essential to finance elections. Most Naga families till date were not prepared to finance a female relative as a candidate from family funds, though the same family would do so for a male. Such kind of unenthusiastic approach towards women and politics was one primary daunting factor for even aspiring Naga women from contesting in elections. Since most women had no economic resources of their own, their aspirations could only be fulfilled if they were backed by a political party. But as experience of general elections in the State have shown, political parties too were not prepared to do so.

While a radical transformation in the existing customary law may not be immediately feasible nor desirable, the State government can use their discretionary power to initiate positive alterations in this regard and can even consider legislative measures which would allow Naga women to inherit at least their parents' acquired property, if not the ancestral property, which would be opposed tooth and nail without a doubt. Legislation along this line could, without radically upsetting the prevailing customary law, facilitate the Naga society to accept the notion of women as equal beneficiaries of parental property. This step would substantially give women a sense of, not only material, but also of social worth. Further, it would play a critical role to boost the confidence of many progressive minded Naga women to take the bold steps towards enhanced political participation. Along the same lines, it becomes imperative to critically re-examine the traditional political system where the Naga women have been associated for long without being either vocal or impressive in number. The cultural marginalization of Naga women from public life have exacted a heavy toll on the all round development of Naga society by not realizing and utilizing the potentialities of the feminine gender in the administration of Naga society for centuries. While the traditional social structure may have been a logical and pragmatic arrangement in the foregone days of constant village raids and headhunting, today, there is no logical reason or explanation for continuing the practice. The present situation in Naga society exemplifies a classic case of the persistence of traditions and customs even though the social and cultural context out of which they emerged are no more. Naga society has nothing to gain by this continued exclusion of women from traditional seats of decision-making and governance of society. On the contrary, this practice effectively loses out on half the valuable human resources of the State, besides projecting the image of the State as one steeped in irrelevant, ancient and primordial social laws. Besides the material aspect of the non-utilization of female human resource, the resultant damage to the confidence and morale of the female population of Naga society by making them voiceless, was indeed the most detrimental factor for impeding the all round development of the Naga women in the State.

Experience of all the general elections in the State bring to light that though women constitute a bulk of the electorate they were not aware of their collective strength, nor has this source been tapped by any political party. Even though international and national laws confer equal rights to women to participate on equal terms with men in all aspects of life, unless local situation of female exclusion from public life is rectified, it would remain a difficult task for the Naga women to enter into the larger male dominated field of politics. It can be safely concurred that Naga women's low accession to political decision-making power was entirely due to the traditional socio-cultural norms and laws, gender stereotypes, attitudes of political parties and society at large, besides women's own internalization of the patriarchal codes and values through a life time of socialization process.

In the larger context of the political empowerment of Naga women the institution of the Church can play a most crucial role. More than half of the women in the State considered the Church to be the most important and relevant institution for Naga women. The importance accorded to the Church by women and the subsequent important role played by the Church in the life of the Naga women clearly indicates that this institution had a direct or indirect influence on the political participation of Naga women. An important offshoot of the Church and its principles on the Naga women was their awakening to women's rights issues. The feminist movement in the North-East region of India was led and nurtured by women who have become aware of the illusions about gender equality in their own societies while undertaking higher studies in the theological discipline. Through the ideological paradigm that had developed to critique the patriarchal structures of the academic world of theological institutions, theologically trained feminists were today questioning the church, its teaching and administrative structures. Despite the gains that have been made by the Christian women in tribal societies in general and the Naga society in particular, the church itself has over the years remained a bastion of male dominance in which women were relegated to a distinctly subordinated position. Thus, the role of the church calls for critical re-examining in the context of its impact on the political participation or non-participation of women. On the one hand, it has undoubtedly opened new vistas for Naga women by providing a sense of self-worth and awareness of their rights, while on the other hand, the church itself propagated and effectively institutionalized a hierarchical structure characterized by male dominance, reflected in its teachings and administrative system. In short, other than the change in nomenclature, a replica of the male-dominated system of governance as that prevail in the villages was instituted within the church. Since the institution of the church occupied a most important place for the Naga women, it had tremendous influence in their role perception affecting their daily life processes. So much so that, even though the church have in many ways awakened the Naga women to their worth as human beings in the Christian perspective, making them conscious of their rights, yet, the teachings, doctrines and structural hierarchy of the church typified patriarchy. This had an indirect impact on their political participation as it served to perpetuate the perceived gender role of being secondary to men, consigned merely to assisting roles. It indirectly restricted their enthusiastic participation in politics because they could not actively seek the leadership roles perceiving it to be a male prerogative. The influence of the church therefore serves to further reinforce the subordinated position of the Naga women in as much the same way as the customary laws did. Given this fact, the church does play an ambivalent role in the empowerment process of Naga women. Since the church is an important and integral part of the social dimensions for the Naga women, it can indeed be considered as one of the most crucial instrument to bring about positive changes for gender-equity in the State. The church, by restructuring its organizational hierarchy and making space for deserving women in its top leadership roles can send a positive message to the society at large to affect similar changes in all forums including the political institutions. The church, it may be noted, is the only institution in Naga society that has the capability to counter the traditional forces, to the extent of quashing customary practices that were deemed inconsistent with the Christian ethics.[8] This fact can be worked to the advantage of advocating for greater political rights for Naga women through sensitization programmes of church leaders and by revisiting the religious norms to exemplify the positive lessons that they can offer society as a whole.

The 2007 annual regional survey carried out by Economic and Social Commission for Asia and the Pacific (ESCAP) concludes that one of the fundamental reasons women are subject to discrimination is that they do not have a voice in decision making at home or in society, even when the matters are directly related to them. The report propounds that gender balance can be achieved at minimum effort and cost provided there is political commitment at the highest levels. Towards this end the State government can play a major role in the political empowerment process of Naga women. The first essential tool for change is the availability of statistics documenting the participation of women and men in public and political life. Statistics are an ideal way to illustrate women's unequal representation in public life. At the State level, this exercise can be carried out by the Department of Women Development, which can make an inventory of public appointments, disaggregated by the gender and the appointing authority, so that it can be clearly seen in which area the shortfall lie. Published routinely, such information would permit women's organizations, concerned NGOs and legislators to put pressure on relevant aspects. The State needs to review and bring positive changes in those aspects of the customary law which are deemed discriminatory towards women. The first step in this direction is for codification of the customary laws, which would make it more amenable to changes as and when social change and situation demanded.

The State can also consider a legislation to limit election expenses which is crucial to allow Naga women into mainstream political arena. One of the foremost reasons that have prevented aspiring Naga women from getting into active politics was because they do not have access to adequate resources and the capital required to fund election campaigns. Further, legislation to increase the number of women on government advisory committees, or public boards is also important to allow more Naga women into decision-making bodies. There can be a mandatory provision that any public committees or boards would not be allowed to be set up until a certain quota of women are nominated or fulfilled.

Planning mechanisms such as quotas or reservation of seats in the local and State legislature must be considered as a short term strategy to hasten the natural, but slow evolution of women into positions of power. In the recent years, adopting positive action measures such as quotas and reserved seats has become a popular and successful tool to promote women in politics. It is crucial to recognize that the central struggle is over power, which is never easily yielded to women candidates by the male incumbents in seats of power. It is possible to give an impetus to the process of political participation of Naga women by creating appropriate interventions at different levels. Studies have shown that countries with lots of women in parliament tend to have quota systems, at least at first. The average level of women in politics in countries with quotas is 20 per cent which is higher than the world's average of women in parliaments that stands at 18.4 per cent.[9] According to the 2009 Global Gender Gap report of the World Economic Forum (WEF) the most gender egalitarian countries on earth includes Finland, Norway, Sweden, and Denmark. Interestingly, all these countries have been using Quotas successfully for many years in various forms, resulting in some of the best democracies of the world. Therefore, reservation should be regarded as a facilitating process that women need.

Voluntary quotas through political parties can also be advocated as an alternative to adopting official quotas for women. In many countries establishing voluntary party quotas has become a first step toward creating gender equality in politics and setting examples for governments and other political institutions in involving women in public life. For instance, in Australia's experience of promoting women in politics, efforts were focused on lobbying political parties to introduce voluntary quotas. The adoption of a voluntary quota by the Australian Labour Party (ALP) in 1994 was a turning point for women in politics in the country. The quota initially called for 35 per cent of women candidates and was later raised to 40 per cent, which in 2008 made it possible for ALP to elect 36 per cent of its women candidates to the Lower House, seats in all Federal State and Territory Parliaments and 37 per cent in the Upper House seats.[10]

Political parties thus can play a most vital function in ensuring greater political participation of Naga women. The role of political parties in determining the prospects for women aspiring to public office cannot be overstated. Towards this end, they can adopt democratic structures by restructuring organizational structure to accommodate women at every level of hierarchy, including the highest levels of decision-making. Political parties must make certain that women are fully represented in party leadership and policy committees. Further, the government can also consider legislation requiring political parties to adopt democratic procedures for their internal operations. The State can provide incentives for political parties to promote women candidates, including resources and training.

Naga women, it has been suggested, need better negotiating skills in order to assume greater public and decision-making roles. Social organizations in the state like women organizations, NGOs and other civil societies have critical roles to play in the upliftment of women by prioritizing women's political empowerment in their own agenda for action. Women's movements and organizations have been one of the key entry points and successful advocacy tools for women candidates entering politics. A number of case studies from around the world, especially from Asia and Africa, indicate that involvement in women's organizations and community works lay the ground for future political involvement by making candidates known for their hard work and dedication to their constituencies. In the Inter-Parliamentary union's survey of 272 parliamentarians from 110 countries, women parliamentarians indicated participation in non-profit organizations and social work as important channels of entry into politics.[11]

Further, women's organizations can play a twofold role by holding their own public awareness campaigns and promoting existing campaigns at the grass-roots level. They can act as the main agents that can inculcate notions of gender-equality and awareness to the Naga women. The emergence of numerous women NGOs and organizations in the State can be regarded as a positive indicator of the growing political consciousness and an awareness of the need to improve and safeguard the position of women. For instance, in the year 2004 a group of Naga women comprising of teachers, media persons, and social workers, who called themselves as 'Facilitators and Initiators' made an effort to field women candidates for the Lok Sabha and Rajya Sabha elections in the State.[12] They came together with the view that Naga women must stop pleading for justice, but must work for and earn justice, well aware of the fact that it would take a very long time for the State Legislative Assembly (an all male bastion) to resolve to legislate women-friendly acts and laws especially in pertaining to power sharing. However, their effort did not succeed in the face of non-cooperation from the existing politicians who failed to extent support for their cause. Further, most of these women being from the elite section of society, had made no effort to garner the support of the general mass of female electorate at the grass-root, who formed the bulk of the electorate. Their very sudden and abrupt way of coming into the electoral scene did not make much impact at the grass root level which played a considerable role in the failure of their stated goal. In fact, creating public awareness through grass-roots organizations and women's groups will lead to a stronger presence of women in the male dominated Naga society.

Women across the State need to organize themselves into organizations, to help them break the barriers of inequality, invisibility and powerlessness. There is the need to build alliances among women's organizations and institutions promoting human rights. Hence, creation of women's networks in business, professions, government, and women's NGOs to create solidarity as well as a sound knowledge base is crucial. Grass-roots organizations can be critical instruments to provide Naga women with collective strength, bargaining capacity and collective articulation of their interests. They can raise women's issues as poll issues, and bargain with political parties and candidates for programmes that are to the advantage of women; provide proper network and support women through nominations and campaign materially, morally and physically. They can also undertake capacity building training for aspiring women leaders to effectively play their role. Another important role that can be played by the women organizations is to identify and promote capable women for election to local, State and national bodies. In this regard, women in senior political positions can reach out to women lower down and promote them to powerful colleagues. Conduct of political awareness programmes, right from the grass-roots level is crucial in creating a more aware women electorate. The efforts of prominent women organizations like the Naga Mothers' Association (NMA) and the other tribal and regional based women's organisations ought to be lauded as they were actively seeking to create political and gender awareness among the women and bring pro-gender changes in society. Based on the understanding that removing restrictions on asset ownership and prioritizing access to resources is vital for achieving gender balance, the 'Watsü Mungdang' is articulating for a change in the customary law whereby females would also be given the right to an equal share in the parents' acquired property. The NMA is currently engaged in awareness programmes on the norms of voting behaviour for women, in an effort to clean up the electoral politics in the State. Active efforts were being made, seeking to create more space for themselves in the largely patriarchal cultural and political set-up through concerted action by way of organizing themselves. These women's organizations have tried to change the prevailing social system by demanding for more rights from 'outside' the political system, because they have not been able to enter the political system, i.e., the State Legislature. However, to effect meaningful and sustainable changes in the social system, Naga women need to act from 'within' the political system, which necessitates that Naga women increase their political participation on all fronts.

Improving the political status of Naga women, besides broadening the political elite structure, is an integral part of the overall problem of socio-economic change of Naga society. Though the present political process in Nagaland remains the exclusive preserve of men, the future of Naga women's participation in public life appeared to be heading in the right direction in light of their growing political consciousness reflected through their emerging perceptions regarding greater representation of women in politics, their gender-awareness, their growing sense of gender justice and not the least, their rising literacy. Given the positive trend towards Naga women's educational attainment and their achievements in other arena besides politics, it is expected that a gender-sensitized and balanced restructuring of the formal institutions in society, both traditional and modern, can alleviate Naga women into positions of equal partnership with men in politics as well as in every aspect of life. It can be stated with certainty that when the female population of the State participates on equal terms with men politically and socially, a truly representative democracy can be realized. Naga women no longer perceived themselves as extensions of men but as individuals with potentialities who can contribute to the societal development. They can do so, provided socio-cultural impediments for their development are removed from their path.

However, enhancement in the social and political awareness of only the women would not suffice to bring positive changes because for any transformation to be affected in society, the entire society, including the men folk needs to be gender-sensitized. The role of men and boys are, therefore, crucial in achieving gender equality. Across the globe today, men are joining women in fighting violence and redefining gender roles. Women cannot progress without the help of men. Enlightened and progressive-minded Naga men need to speak out against practices that are deemed gender-biased and discriminatory with the knowledge that in the Naga society the voice of one man is equivalent to the voice of a hundred women. The concept of masculinity as that of power or control must be redefined in Naga society and elsewhere. In many societies images of violence against women in media are associated with sexual power and virility. Alternative models of masculinity that encompass respect for women should be encouraged.

Without a change in the consciousness of the entire society, no social transformation will be able to set women free of their inhibitions that have crystallized over the ages. Naga women are highly educated, politically as well as socially conscious, aware of their rights and progressive looking. Yet, despite all these factors in their favour, they remain voiceless, and unable to break through the male dominance in the society in general, and in the political sphere in particular. The concept of femininity must, therefore, incorporate strength. Naga women must value their femininity—but they must also gain strength and courage. Courage to achieve equality, courage to fight for their rights, courage to speak out against discrimination and courage to change society for the better.

REFERENCES

1. Jamir, Toshimenla, '*Political Consciousness and Participation of Naga Women: A Sociological Enquiry*' (Ph.D. Thesis), Nagaland University 2007.
2. Congress President's Address, '*Shimla Sankalp*', Shimla-Himachal, July 7-9, 2003.
3. This step was reportedly affected at the insistence of the Congress President Mrs. Sonia Gandhi. Since then two women representatives are included in the list of AICC representation from the State as of October 2010.
4. 'Gaon Bura' literally means a 'village elder', or amongst some tribes with chieftainship system of polity, it refers to the village chief. In the present context, a 'Gaon Bura' assists the district administration in the governance of society.
5. Resolution taken in the Nagaland GB Federation General Sessions Meeting, 14th October, 2010.
6. Horam, M., *Naga Polity*, New Delhi, 1975, pp. 77-78.
7. Jamir, Toshimenla, No.1.
8. There are many instances where the institution of the Church in Nagaland has prevailed over traditional practices. One of such is the reduction in the period of mourning on the death of a Naga. Traditionally in the Ao Naga Tribe, when a men died, six days of mourning period was observed, whereas for a women only five days mourning period was the norm. On the directive of the Apex Church body, a mourning period of three days is uniformly observed for both men and women today. Traditional bodies such as the Village Councils could not oppose the church directive to this effect.

9. Quotas by Country; Quota Project. http://www.quotaproject.org/country.cfm
10. Rodrigues, Charmaine, Comment on the Affirmative Action Measure in the Pacific Region, 2008. http://www.iknowpolitics.org/en/node/5827#comment-2119.
11. Ballington, J., Equality in Politics: A survey of Women and Men in Parliaments, Inter-Parliamentary Union (IPU), 2008. http://www.iknowpolitics.org/en/node/5415
12. *Nagaland Post*: Women to field candidates for Nagaland LS and RS Seats, 16th March, 2004.

Bibliography

Agarwal, Bina, "From Mexico 1975 to Beijing 1995", *Indian Journal of Gender Studies*, Vol. 3, No. 1, 1996, pp. 87-92.

Agnihotri, Indu, "The Fourth World Conference on Women: A Report from China", *Indian Journal of Gender Studies*, Vol. 3, No. 1, January-June, 1996, pp. 111-125.

Almond, G., Sidney Verba, *The Civic Culture*, Princeton: Princeton University Press, 1963.

Andal, N., *Women and Indian Society—Options and Constraints*, Jaipur: Rawat Publications, 2002.

Ao, A. Lanunungsang, "Working System of Tsuki: A traditional female institution of the Ao-Nagas", *Nagaland University Research Journal*, Vol. 1, September 2003, pp. 130-35.

Ao, Tajen, *Ao Naga Customary Laws*, Mokokchung, 1980.

Ao, Tajenyuba, *Ao Naga Customary Laws*, Mokokchung, 1957.

Arya, Rashmi, *Women in Public Sector*, New Delhi: Manak Publications Pvt. Ltd., 1990.

Ashworth, Georgina, *Women are not Half Human: An Overview of Women's Rights*, London: Third World Foundation for Social and Economic Studies, 1985.

Avasthi, Abha, A.K. Srivastava, (ed.), *Modernity, Feminism and Women Empowerment*, Jaipur: Rawat Publications.

Ballington, J., Equality in Politics: A Survey of Women and Men in Parliaments, Inter-Parliamentary Union (IPU), 2008. *http://www.iknowpolitics.org/en/node/5415*

Bareh, H.M., *Encyclopedia of North-East India*, Vol. VI, New Delhi: Mittal Publications, 2001.

Baud, I.S.A., *Forms of Production and Women's Labour: Gender Aspects of Industrialization in India and Mexico*, New Delhi: Sage Publications India Pvt. Ltd, 1992.

Beauvoir, Simone de, *The Second Sex*, Harmondsworth: Penguin, 1972.

Bhatt, Shanta, *Women Parliamentarians of India*, Udaipur: Shiva Publishers Distributors, 1995.

Bhelanda, Anjali and Mala Pandurag, (ed.), *Articulating Gender*, New Delhi: Pencraft International, 2000.

Bhowmik, K.L., (ed.), *Current Anthropological and Archaeological Perspectives*, Vol. II: Society and Culture, New Delhi: Inter India Publications, 1985.

Bhuyan, B.C., *The Tribal Women*, New Delhi: Omsons Publications, 1993.

Boserup, E., *Women's Role in Economic Development*, London: George and Unwin, 1970.

Bulbeck, Chilla, "Articulating Structure and Agency: How Women's Studies Students express their relationship with Feminism", *Women's Studies International Forum*, Vol. 24, No. 2, 2001, pp. 141-155, Elsevier Science Ltd, New York.

Carr, Marilyn, Martha Chen, Renana Jhabvala, *Speaking Out: Women's Economic Empowerment in South-East Asia*, New Delhi: Vistaar Publications, 1997.

Census of India 2001, Nagaland, Directorate of Census Operations, Kohima. Indian National Congress (I) Election Manifesto General Election, 1996. Manifesto for Election to Lok Sabha 2004, Democratic Alliance of Nagaland. *Nagaland Basic Facts 2003*, Kohima, Nagaland.

Census of India 2011, Provisional Population Totals, Nagaland Series 14, Directorate of Census Operations, Kohima, Nagaland.

Chasie, Charles, *The Naga Imbroglio*, Kohima: Standard Printers and Publishers, 1999.

Chatterji, Shoma A., *The Indian Women's Search for Identity*, New Delhi: Vikas Publishing House Pvt. Ltd., 1988.

Chopra, J.K., *Women in the Indian Parliament*, New Delhi: Mittal Publications, 1993.

Clark, Mead, *Ao Naga Women*, Boston, 1896.

Dahl, R., *Who Governs?* New Haven: Yale University Press, 1981.

Dahl, Robert A., *Modern Political Analysis*, New Delhi: Prentice Hall of India Pvt. Ltd, 1997.

Das, Bibekenanda, L.N., Dash, *The Feminine Gender*, New Delhi: Manak Publications Pvt. Ltd,, 1995.

David, L., (ed.), *International Encyclopaedia of Social Sciences*, Vol. 13, New York: Macmillan and Free Press, 1972.

Downs, Anthony, *An Economic Theory of Democracy*, New York: Harper & Bros, 1957.

Downs, Frederick S., *The Christian Impact on The Status of Women in North-East India*, Shillong: NEHU Publications, 1996.

Dreze, Jean, Amartya Sen, *India: Development and Participation*, New Delhi: Oxford University Press, 2002.

Dutta, R.K., *Women Empowerment*, New Delhi: Reference Press, 2003.

Ganguli, Milada, *A Pilgrimage to the Nagas*, New Delhi: Oxford and IBJ publishing Co., 1984.

Gariyali, C.K., *Inching Forward: Political Empowerment of Women in Commonwealth Countries*, New Delhi: Vitri Publishers, 1999.

Gathia, Joseph, "Beijing Agenda: A New Commitment", *Mainstream*, September 30, 1995, pp. 13-17.

Ghadially, Rehana, (ed.), *Women in Indian Society*, New Delhi: Sage Publications, 1988.

Ghose, Malini, "Literacy, Power and Feminism" *Economic and Political Weekly*, April 27, 2002, pp. 1615-1620.

Ghosh, B.B., *History of Nagaland*, New Delhi: 1983.

Ghosh, G.K., *Tribals and their Culture* ,Vol. 3: *Manipur and Nagaland*, New Delhi: Ashish Publishing House, 1995.

Giri, V. Mohini, *Emancipation and Empowerment of Women*, New Delhi: Gyan Publishing House, 1998.

Goonatilake, Hema, "Status of Women" *Proceedings Asahi International, Symposium Women in Changing World*, October 23-25, 1985, pp. 15-20, (Tokyo).

Gradodol, David and Joan Swan, *Gender Voices*, Massachusetts: Blackwell, 1995.

Guha, Sampa, *Political Participation of Women in Changing Society*, New Delhi, Inter-India Publications, 1996.

Gupta, Asha, "Women, Power and Culture", *Employment News*, March 22-28, 1997, pp. 1-2.

Haimendorf, Von Christoph, *The Naked Nagas*, London: Methuen & Co, 1939.

Halch, Afshar (ed.), *Women and Empowerment: Illustrations from the Third World*, London: Macmillan Press Ltd, 1988.

Hnuni, R.L., *Transforming Theology for Empowering Women*, Jorhat: Eastern Theological College, 1999.

Horam, M., *Naga Polity*, New Delhi: B.R. Publishing Corporation, 1975.

Horam, M., *Social and Cultural life of the Nagas*, New Delhi: Low Price Publications, 1977.

Hutton, J.H., *The Angami Nagas*, Bombay: Oxford University Press, 1969.

Imchen, Panger, *Ancient Ao Naga religion and Culture*, New Delhi: Har-Anand Publications, 1993.

Imkonglemba, "Revitalisation and reorganisation of rural development programmes in Nagaland", *Kurukshetra*, December 1995, pp. 29-34.

International Encyclopaedia of Sociology, Vol. 2, London: Fitzroy Dearborn Publishers, 1995.

Jacobs, Julian, *The Nagas: Hill Peoples of North East India*, London: Thames & Hudson Ltd, 1998.

Jacobsen, Joyce P., *The Economics of Gender*, Oxford: Blackwell Publishers Ltd., 1994.

Jain, Devaki, *Women's Quest for Power*, Ghaziabad: Vikas Publishing House Pvt. Ltd., 1980.

Jain, P., Maha Rajen, (ed.), *Women Images*, New Delhi: Rawat Publications, 1996.

Jaiswal, R.P., *Professional Status of Women*, Jaipur: Rawat Publications, 1993.

Jaitley, Jaya, "Another Side of Politics", *Indian Journal of Gender Studies*, Vol. 3, No. 2, 1996, pp. 269-274.

Jamir, Imnukshila, "Role of Women in Rural Development Programme in the State", *A Decade of the SIRD, 2000*, Government of Nagaland, pp. 53-55.

Jamir, N. Talitemjen and A. Lanunungsang, *Naga Society and Culture*, Mokokchung: Nagaland University, Tribal Research Centre, 2005.

Jenks, Chris, *Culture*, London: Routledge, 1993.

Jodi, Dean, (ed.), *Feminism and the New Democracy*, New Delhi: Sage Publications India Pvt Ltd, 1997.

Johnstone, J., *Manipur and the Naga Hills*, New Delhi, 1971.

Joseph, John, "Inter-Parliamentary specialized Conference on: Towards Partnership between Men and Women in Politics—An Overview",

The Journal of Parliamentary Information, Vol. XVIII, No. 1, March 1997, pp. 17-47.

Kalbagh, Chetana, *Women and Development*, New Delhi: Discovery Publishing House, 1991.

Kannabiran, Vasanth and Kalpam Kannabiram, "From Social Action to Political Action: Women and the 81st Amendment", *Economic and Political Weekly*, February 1, 1997, pp. 196-197.

Kanshik, Susheela, (ed.), *Women's Oppression, Patterns and Perspectives*, New Delhi: Shakti Books, 1985.

Kant, Anjani, *Women and the Law*, New Delhi: A.P.H. Publishing Corporation, 1997.

Karlekar, Hiranmay, "Miles to go for a Fair Representation", *Indian Journal of Gender Studies*, Vol. 3, No. 2, 1996, pp. 175-281.

Kasturi, L., Vina Mazumdar, *Women and Indian Nationalism*, New Delhi: Vikas Publishing House Pvt Ltd, 1994.

Kaushall, Ranchana, *Women and Human Rights in India*, New Delhi: Kaveri Books, 2000.

Kikon, Dolly, "Political Mobilization of Women in Nagaland: A Sociological Background" *NPMHR Quarterly Publication*, Vol. 6, No. 01, April 2002, pp. 11-14.

Kiremwati, *Education and the Nagas*, Kohima: 1995.

Koehn, Daryl, *Rethinking Feminist Ethics*, London: Routledge, 1998.

Kuba Joseph, "Re-Situating Narratives" *NPMHR Occasional Publication*, Winter of 2000-2001, pp. 4-5.

Kumari, Ranjana, (ed.), *Women in Decision Making*, New Delhi: Vikas Publishing House Pvt. Ltd., 1997.

Lee, Jungja, "Women's Political Representation in South Korea: Structural Response" *Korea Observer*, Vol. XXII, No. 1, 1991, pp. 537-553 (Seoul: The Institute of Korean Studies).

Lennie, June, "Deconstructing Gendered Power Relations in Participatory Planning: Towards an empowering feminist framework of participation and action" *Women's Studies International Forum*, Vol. 22, No. 1, 1999, pp. 97-110, Elsevier Science, New York.

Leo, K.S. Paul, "Naga Women and Human Rights" *Raisunriang*, 4th Issue, 1998, pp. 7-21.

Lerner, Gerda, *The Creation of Patriarchy*, New York: Oxford University Press, 1986.

Lithui, Shimreichon, "Women for Peace in Nagalim" *NPMHR Occasional Publication*, Winter of 2000-2001, pp. 3-4.

Longchar, Imtilemla, *Portrayal of Women in Drama*, Dimapur, 1999.

Loutfi, Martha Fetherolf, (ed.), *Women, Gender and Work*, Jaipur: Rawat Publications, 2002.

Mahanta, Ananda, *Study of Human Culture*, Guwahati: Omsons Publications, 1987.

Mahapatra, Subhasini, *Women and Politics*, New Delhi: Rajat Publications, 2001.

Mahapatra, Subhasini, *Women Participation in Labour Force*, New Delhi: Rajat Publications, 2002.

Mainstreaming Gender, *http://www.un.org.womenwatch/osagi/gender/mainstreaming.htm*

Maithreyi, K., R.M. Sudarshan, A. Shariff, *Gender, Population and Development*, New Delhi: Oxford University Press, 1999.

Majumdar, P.K., R.P., Kataria, *The Constitution of India*, Allahabad: Orient Publishing Company, 1996.

Manchanda, Rita, (ed.), *Women, War and Peace in South Asia*, New Delhi: Sage Publications India Pvt. Ltd., 2001.

Mazumdar, Vina, *"The Non-Aligned Movement and the International Women's Decade: A Summary of Decisions"*, Center for Women's Studies, New Delhi, 8th March, 1983.

Menon, Nivedita, (ed.), *Gender and Politics in India*, New Delhi: Oxford University Press, 1999.

Meru, K., "The Role of Women before and Now" *Highlander*, Vol. III, No. 2, September 1975, pp. 18-23.

Milbrath, L., *Political Participation: How and Why People get involved in Politics*? Chicago: Rand McNally & Co., 1965.

Mills, J.P., *The Ao Nagas*, Bombay: Oxford University Press, 1973.

Misra, R.P., *Research Methodology*, New Delhi: Concept Publishing Company, 1989.

Modi, Milorai, "Participation of Women in Grasswork Politics: A Case Study of Adis Women", *Arunachal University Research Journal*, Vol. 5 (2), 2002, pp. 47-55.

Mukhopadhyay, Lili, *Tribal Women in Development*, New Delhi: Ministry of Information and Broadcasting, Government of India, 2002.

Mullick, S. Bosu, "Indigenous Peoples' Experience with Electoral and Party Politics in India", Paper presented in *Asian Regional Workshop*, July 14-16, 2000, Sabah, Malaysia.

Neelson, John P., *Gender, Caste and Power in South Asia: Status and Mobility in a Transitional Society*, New Delhi: Manohar Publications, 1991.

Noris, Pippa, *Democratic Phoenix: Reinventing Political Activism*, Cambridge: Cambridge University Press, 2002.

Noris, Pippa, J. Lovenduski, R. Campbell, "*Women's Political Participation in the UK*", 2005. http://www.electoralcommission.org.uk/

Nussbaum, C. Martha, *Women and Development: The Capabilities Approach*, New Delhi: Kali for Women, 2000.

Oppong, Christine and Katherine Abu, *A Handbook for Data Collection and Analysis on Seven Roles and Statutes of Women*, Geneva: International Labour Office, 1988.

Ostergaard, Lise, (ed.), *Gender and Development: A Practical Guide*, London: Routledge Publication, 1992.

Panda, Snehlata, *Determinants of Political Participation: Women and Public Activity*, New Delhi: Ajanta Publications, 1990.

Pandy, Suman, *Women in Politics*, Jaipur: Rawat Publications, 1990.

Partners in Human Development, United Nations Development Programme, New York,2003.

Patel, Vibhuti, *Women's Challenges of the New Millennium*, New Delhi: Gyan Publishing House, 2002.

Payne, Geoff, (ed.), *Social Divisions*, New York: Palgrave, 2000.

Peterson, V. Spike, "The Politics of Identification in the Context of Globalization", *Women Studies International Forum*, Vol. 19, 1996, New York, pp. 5-15.

Peterson, V. Spike, "Women and Gender in Power/Politics, Nationalism and Revolution", *Journal of Politics*, Vol. 57, No. 2, pp. 870-78, May 1995, Austin: University of Texas Press.

Phadnis, Urmila and Indira Malani, *Women of the World—Illusion and Reality*, New Delhi: Vikas Publishing House Pvt. Ltd., 1978.

Phillipose, Pamela, "The Women's Vote: Manifestoes of Hypocrisy", *Indian Journal of Gender Studies*, Vol. 3, No. 2, 1996, pp. 261-264.

Phukon, Giri, (ed.), *Political Dynamics of North-East India*, New Delhi: South Asia Publishers, 2000.

Pujari, Premlata, Vijay Kumari Kaushik, *Women Power in India,* Vol. 3, *Women's Development Work and Framework*, New Delhi: Kenosha Publishers and Distributors, 1994.

Putnam, Robert, *Bowling Alone: The Collapse and Revival of American Community*, New York: Simon & Schuster, 2000.

Quotas by Country; Quota Project. http://www.quotaproject.org/country.cfm

Rajput, Pam and Swarup, Hemlata, *Women and Globalization: Reflections, Options and Strategies*, New Delhi: Ashish Publication House, 1994.

Ramegowda, A., *Gender Inequality*, Jaipur: Rawat Publishers, 1997.

Rao, Nitya, "Empowerment through Organization: Women Workers in the Informal Sector", *Indian Journal of Gender Studies,* Vol. 3, No. 2, 1996, pp. 171-197.

Raphael, Dana, *Being Female: Reproduction, Power and Change*, Hague: Mounton Publishers, 1975.

Report of the Eighth General Assembly Election to the Nagaland Legislative Assembly 1993, Government of Nagaland.

Report on the Seventh General Election to the Nagaland Legislative Assembly 1988-89, Government of Nagaland.

Report on the Sixth General Election to the Nagaland Legislative Assembly 1987, Government of Nagaland.

Report on the Tenth General Election to the Nagaland Legislative Assembly 2003, Government of Nagaland.

Result of the General Assembly Election of Nagaland (Fifth Edition), Government of Nagaland, Kohima, 2004.

Robinson, V., D. Richardson, (ed.), *Introducing Women's Studies*, London: Macmillan, 1997.

Rodriques, Charmaine, *Comment on the Affirmative Action Measure in the Pacific Region, 2008.* http://www.iknowpolitics.org/en/node/5827#comment-2119

Routledge International Encyclopaedia of Women, New York: Routledge Publishers, 2000.

Rush, M., P. Althoff, *An Introduction to Political Sociology*, London: Nelson, 1971.

Rustagi, Preet, "Significance of Gender-related Development Indicators: An Analysis of Indian States" *Indian Journal of Gender Studies*, Vol. 11, No. 3, 2004, pp. 291-337.

Sahay, B.N., "Nagaland experiment with decentralization", *Kurukshetra* March 1989, pp. 39-42.

Sarkar Mahua, "Looking for Feminism", *Gender and History*, Vol. 16, No. 2, August 2004, pp. 318-27, Oxford: Blackwell Publishing Ltd.

Sarkar, Lotika and Sivaramayya, (ed.), *Women and Law: Contemporary Problems*, New Delhi: Vikas Publishing House Pvt. Ltd., 1994.

Sema, Piketo Dr., *British Policy and Administration in Nagaland 1881-1947*, New Delhi: Scholar Publishing House, 1992.

Sen, Amartya, *Inequality Re-examined*, New Delhi: Oxford University Press, 1992.

Sen, Amartya, *Reason before Identity*, New Delhi: Oxford University Press, 1999.

Seth, Mira, *Women and Development*, New Delhi: Sage Publications India Pvt. Ltd., 2001.

Sethi, Raj Mohini, (ed.), *Globalization, Culture and Women's Development*, Jaipur: Rawat Publications, 1999.

Shangkham, Gina, "Naga Women and Peace Process" *NPMHR Occasional Publication*, Winter of 2000-2001, pp. 1 and 8.

Sharma, Kumud, "Gender, Environment and Structural Adjustment", *Economic and Political Weekly*, April 30, 1994, pp. 5-11.

Sharma, Kumud, "Transformative Politics: Dimensions of Women's Participation in Panchayati Raj", *Indian Journal of Gender Studies*, Vol. 5, No. 1, January-June, 1998, pp. 23-47.

Sharma, Kumud, Sabha Hussain and Archana, *Women in Focus: A Community in Search of Equal Roles*, Hyderabad: Sangam Books Pvt. Ltd., 1984.

Sharma, R.C., *Gender Profile of Nagaland*, New Delhi: UNESCO, 2001.

Shashi, S.S., *The Tribal Women of India*, New Delhi: Swadesh Pra Dad Singhal, 1978.

Shimla Sankalp (Congress President's Opening and Closing Address), 7-9 July 2003, Shimla, Himachal Pradesh.

Shimmi, Y.L. Roland, *Comparative History of the Nagas, from Ancient Period till 1826*, New Delhi: Inter India Publications, 1988.

Shishak, Tuisem A., "Nagas and Education", *Nagas' 90*, 1990, pp. 22-35.

Sinha, A.C., Pariyam M. Chacko, I.L. Aier, *Hill Cities of Eastern Himalayas*, New Delhi: Indus Publishing Company, 1993.

Sitterly, Connie and Beth Whitley Duke, *A Woman's Place: Management*, New Jersey: Prentice Hall, Englewood Cliffs, 1988.

Smelser, Neil J. (ed.), *Handbook of Sociology*, California: Sage Publications Inc., 1989.

Smith, W.C., *The Ao-Naga Tribes of Assam*, Delhi: Gian Publications, 1957.

Soin, Kanwaljit, "Why Women, What Politics", Centre for Asia-Pacific Women in Politics. http://www.capwip.org/resources/soin/soinpaper.html

Sood, Rita, *Changing Status and Adjustment of Women*, New Delhi: Manak Publications, 1995.

Statistical Handbook of Nagaland 2001, Government of Nagaland, Kohima.

Statistical Handbook of Nagaland 2003, Government of Nagaland, Kohima.

Sweeney, Belinda, "Trans-ending Women's Rights: The Politics of Trans-inclusion in the age of gender", *Women's Studies International Forum*, 27, 2004, pp. 75-88, Elsevier, Singapore.

Takatemjen, *Studies on Theology and Naga Culture*, Mokokchung: 1997.

Tenth Five Year Plan 2002-2007, Planning and Co-ordination Department, Nagaland.

Terhuja, K., "Status of Women in Naga Society", *Nagas' 90*, 1990, pp. 18-21.

Thakur, Rashmi, "Women and Political Empowerment", *Employment News*, June 24-30, 2000, pp. 1-3.

The Polity Reader in Gender Studies, Oxford: Blackwell Publishers Ltd., 2002.

Thomas, C. Joshua, Gurudas Das, (ed.), *Dimensions of Development in Nagaland*, New Delhi: Regency Press, 2002.

Tinker, Irene, (ed.), *Persistent Inequalities—Women and World Development*, New York: Oxford University Free Press, Inc., 1990).

Tripathy, Swarnamayee, *Political Participation of Women Workers in India*, New Delhi: Vikas Publishing House Pvt. Ltd., 2000.

Ueno, Chizuko, "Femininity and Masculinity" Proceedings Asahi International, *Symposium on Women in Changing World*, October 23-25, 1998 pp. 67-71, (Tokyo).

UNDP Human Development Report 1994, New Delhi: UNDP Publications, 1994.

United Nations Declaration on the Elimination of Violence against Women, http://www.unhchr.ch/

Upadhyay, H.C., *Status of Women in India*, New Delhi: Anmol Publications, 1991.

Varma, S.P., *Modern Political Theory*, New Delhi: Vikas Publishing House Pvt. Ltd., 1998.

Varma, Sudhir, *Women's Struggle for Political Space*, Jaipur: Rawat Publications, 1997.

Vashum, R., Aleube Iheilung, Nehemiah Panmei, Lanu Longkumer, (ed.), *Nagas At Work*, New Delhi: NSUD Publication, 1996.

Vidya, K.C., *Political Empowerment of Women at the Grassroots*, New Delhi: Kanishka Publishers, 1997.

Wazir, Rekha, *The Gender Gap in Basic Education*, New Delhi: Sage Publications, 2000.

Workshop on Policy and Strategy of Rural Development Progress in Nagaland, March 3-4, 1995, Department of Rural Development, Kohima.

"Weaving Illusions"!, Grassroots Options, Spring 2002.

"Women Power", *Newsweek*, March 9, 1992.

Xaxa, Virginius, "Women and Gender in the Study of Tribes in India", *Indian Journal of Gender Studies*, Vol. 11, No. 3, 2004, pp. 345-367.

Yadav, R.J., *Women Entrepreneurship*, Rajkot: Poorvi Press Ltd., 1999.

Zarnowska, Anna, "Women's Political Participation in Inter-War Poland: Opportunities and Limitations" *Women History Review* Vol. 13, No. 1, 2004, pp. 57-67, Portsmouth: Triangle Journals Ltd., Websites

Zehol, Lucy, (ed.), *Women in Naga Society*, New Delhi: Regency Publications, 1998.

Index